With much spi̇ _____ y
heard my goo _____ e
biblical, doctrina̱, ⌣⌢⌣⌣⌣⌣⌣⌣, _____ ̣e
Beatitudes in Matthew 5. In decades past, he has on more
than one occasion shared with me the insights that God has
provided to him as he meditated frequently and deeply on
this precious portion of Jesus' teaching. For these reasons and
more, I am so grateful that he has written out these messages
in full so that many more may profit from them. If you want
a basic, edifying book that provides a scriptural paradigm
of genuine experiential Christianity flowing from the teach-
ings of our Lord, I would recommend this little gem. Read
it slowly, meditatively, and prayerfully. May the Lord of the
Beatitudes make it a great blessing to you.

—Dr. Joel R. Beeke, president of Puritan Reformed
Theological Seminary and a pastor of the Heritage
Reformed Congregation, Grand Rapids, Michigan

Experiential Christianity is not a mystical experience but
rather the experience of the liberating and transforming
power of Christ's truths in a person's life. The ultimate purpose of salvation is to conform the sinner to the image of Jesus
Christ. The portraits of the regenerated heart and sanctified
life that Jesus masterfully and pastorally summed up in these
seven sketches of the new-born soul are faithfully, practically,
and searchingly expounded by the author. The insights of this
work about the internal structure and interrelatedness of the
Beatitudes will be a unique contribution to other commen-
taries on the Beatitudes. The author's instructions regarding
these perspectives nearly thirty years ago have benefited me
for many years in my preaching and pastoral ministry. I am

thankful that by way of this book, these instructions will have wider publicity. I am hopeful that this teaching will enrich many other laborers in the Word as well as yield the experience of the blessedness of being in Christ.

—Rev. Arnoud T. Vergunst, pastor of the Netherlands Reformed Congregation, Waupun, Wisconsin

My friend and brother, Bart Elshout, has preached a series of messages about the Sermon on the Mount. In this important discourse, Jesus sets forth the standards of His kingdom and gives a description of His true subjects. Rev. Elshout has the gift to bring Christ's message close to our hearts. As always, his exegesis is thorough, and it includes the necessary call to self-examination. Christianity is a religion that must be lived and practiced—a matter of paramount importance to Rev. Elshout—which I have observed as a reflection of the influence of his God-fearing father and mother. I wholeheartedly recommend this book.

—Rev. Cornelis Harinck, pastor of the Reformed Congregations in the Netherlands since 1962

With boldness, clarity and warmth, Pastor Elshout passionately expounds the biblical, spiritual and experiential truths of the Beatitudes. He is a gifted preacher that skillfully makes the written Word of God understandable to young and old with fitting applications. At numerous times he lovingly reminds us from the pulpit that the written Word leads us to the Living Word, the Lord Jesus Christ. We highly recommend his series of sermons on the Beatitudes.

—Consistory of the Heritage Reformed Congregation, Hull, Iowa

CHRIST'S PORTRAIT
OF THE CHRISTIAN

CHRIST'S PORTRAIT OF THE CHRISTIAN

An Exposition of the Beatitudes

BARTEL ELSHOUT

BIBLICAL SPIRITUALITY PRESS

Biblical Spirituality Press
biblicalspiritualitypress.org
biblicalspiritualitypress@gmail.com

Printed in the United States of America
ISBN: 978-0-9889498-5-0

CONTENTS

PREFACE

At the suggestion and urging of my beloved son-in-law and fellow minister of the gospel, Rev. Brian Najapfour, I have prepared my series of sermons about the Beatitudes for print. The subject addressed in this book is dear to my heart, and I use it frequently as a paradigm for pastoral discussions regarding the essentials of Christian experience.

In expounding the riches of Christ's portrait of the Christian, I am endeavoring to follow in the footsteps of my beloved father, the late Rev. Arie Elshout (1923–1991), who in each of the seven churches he served would always begin his preaching ministry with an exposition of the Beatitudes. He did so to lay the scriptural groundwork for the experiential dimension of his preaching as well as for his pastoral ministry. I have done likewise in the three churches I have been privileged to serve: the Heritage Reformed Congregation of Jordan, Ontario (1998–2005), the Heritage Reformed Congregation of Chilliwack, British Columbia (2005–2012), and my current charge, the Heritage Reformed Congregation of Hull, Iowa (2016–present).

However, my first attempt to expound the Beatitudes occurred during my engagement as an evangelist in Denver, Colorado (1984–1989). As I began to proclaim God's Word there, emphasizing its experiential dimension and application, those in attendance increasingly began to ask me to explain the essentials of Christian experience. I realized the importance of responding scripturally to such inquiries, and this prompted me to make this a matter of much prayer. The Lord graciously answered that prayer by increasingly shedding light on the Beatitudes and their remarkable structure. This inspired me to launch my first exposition of the spiritual traits of God's children set forth in Christ's sevenfold portrait.

This book represents my most recent exposition of the Beatitudes in my current congregation, the Heritage Reformed Congregation of Hull, Iowa. Having prepared this exposition for publication, I am keenly aware that I am making but a minor contribution to the extensive and excellent body of literature already available on this subject, to which I am very much indebted.

Having said that, however, I am hopeful that God will be pleased to use this little work for instruction and edification. It is my prayer that the Author of this spiritual portrait of His people, our blessed Lord Jesus Christ, may be honored and magnified by this attempt to set forth His infinite wisdom articulated in the Beatitudes. In short, may this exposition of the written Word lead us to the Living Word, whose riches are unsearchable!

In conclusion, I wish to acknowledge all who have contributed to the publication of this treatise. First, I wish to thank my son-in-law, Rev. Brian Najapfour, for stimulating me to publish this treatise on the occasion of my seventieth birthday, and for always challenging me to think creatively about being engaged in the ministry to which Christ has so graciously called me. I also thank him for his careful and competent review of the content of this treatise. I count it a privilege to be his co-laborer in God's kingdom!

My heartfelt thanks also to all who have contributed to preparing this treatise for print: Gina Bessetti-Reyes for her initial editing of my transcribed sermons, Andrew Buss for his expert editing in preparing my spoken words for publication, Amy Zevenbergen for her design of a beautiful and fitting cover, and my dear friends of many years, Linda and Gary den Hollander, for their expert typesetting.

My loving thanks also to my beloved wife, Clarice, for faithfully and prayerfully supporting me in the ministry of the gospel and for encouraging me to prepare this treatise for print—and to my late wife, Joan, who may now be filled with that for which she hungered and thirsted: Christ and His righteousness.

Finally, and most importantly, I am deeply indebted to the Lord Jesus Christ, my inexpressibly precious Savior, for sovereignly calling even a man such as I am to be His ambassador in a fallen world. My indebtedness to Him cannot be expressed in words! All glory therefore be to the Father's well-beloved Son, whose I am and whom I may serve.

Bartel Elshout
Inwood, Iowa
February 2019

THE FIRST SEVEN BEATITUDES: A PERFECT DESCRIPTION

In Matthew 4 we read that Jesus went about all Galilee teaching in synagogues and preaching the gospel of the kingdom. Neither before nor since has anyone preached the gospel in such an extraordinary fashion. After all, the Lord Jesus Christ Himself is the embodiment of the gospel—the glad tidings of the Living Word of God (John 1:1).

What a profoundly unique experience it must have been to be in His audience—to hear the Living Word of God expounding His own written word! Such was the privilege of the multitude that heard Him explain the Old Testament Scriptures that He had inspired by His Spirit, an exposition commonly known as the Sermon on the Mount (Matthew 5–7).

Before we explore the opening verses of this sermon (Matt. 5:3–9), we need to recognize Jesus' intention and purpose for preaching it. We need to remember that the great mission for which His Father had sent Him into the world was always foremost on His mind (John 3:17; 4:34). During His earthly ministry, He was profoundly conscious of the fact that He had come into this world to seek and to save that which was lost (Luke 19:10) and to give His life as a ransom for many (Matt. 20:28).

The Sermon on the Mount derives its name from the location where Christ preached it, on a slight elevation on the northwestern shore of the Sea of Galilee. Thus, positioning Himself so that His audience could hear Him well, the Lord Jesus Christ began to deliver this remarkable sermon, the lengthiest of His recorded discourses in the New Testament. Although it is commonly referred to as the greatest sermon ever preached, there appears to be a prevailing misunderstanding regarding His objective in preaching it. Some maintain that Jesus' only objective was to provide His audience with in-depth instruction regarding biblical morality. Although there is much instruction in this sermon about biblical morality (the spirituality of the moral law), Christ had a far more compelling motive.

As we stated earlier, "the Son of man is come to seek and to save that which was lost" (Luke 19:10). Thus, when Jesus walked among men and addressed an audience, He was profoundly aware of being surrounded by perishing sinners who needed to believe on Him for their salvation. Sadly, the majority of His countrymen were oblivious to their need. They were unaware that their entire conduct failed to measure up to God's standard of impeccable righteousness.

To capture their attention, the Lord Jesus made a bold pronouncement in Matthew 5:20: "Except your righteousness shall exceed the righteousness of the scribes and Pharisees, ye shall in no case enter into the kingdom of heaven." This was a stunning statement indeed! The ignorant and misguided people whom He was addressing believed that their spiritual leaders—the Pharisees and scribes—had achieved the highest level of spirituality and were the ultimate standard of righteousness. Now Jesus tells them that their righteousness falls short of God's impeccable standard. He confronts them with the unsettling truth that if they have nothing better than the flawed righteousness of the scribes and Pharisees, they will not enter the kingdom of heaven. As Jesus progresses in the proclamation of this sermon, He begins to expound the law of God. He does so for one purpose: to confront these sons and daughters of Abraham with the fact that they were transgressors of the law. Why was this so necessary?

Unless they perceived themselves as transgressors, they would never understand their need of a savior. Jesus therefore goes beyond the letter of the law and sets before them the spirituality of the law. He did so, for instance, by saying, "Ye have heard that it was said by them of old time, Thou shalt not commit adultery: But I say unto you, That whosoever looketh on a woman to lust after her hath committed adultery with her already in his heart" (Matt. 5:27–28).

Having been taught erroneously by the scribes and Pharisees, these people believed that as long as one observes the letter of the law—as long as one's life is in order outwardly—all is well. The Lord Jesus therefore zeroes in on this erroneous teaching by saying (and I paraphrase), "Though you may have heard this from your teachers, let Me now tell you what the law really means." He wanted them to recognize that to be righteous before God, their inner motives and inclinations needed to conform perfectly to His law.

The Christ who is speaking here is none other than the Lawgiver Himself. As the Angel of the covenant, He spoke at Mount Sinai and gave the law to His people in Israel (Acts 7:38). As the Lawgiver, Christ is thus expounding His own law to these men and women, who needed to understand that in their innermost being they were law breakers.

Only when we understand this experientially will we understand our need for a savior. Only then will we value a gospel that proclaims the glad tidings that we have a savior who, on behalf of law breakers such as ourselves, has obeyed His own law perfectly, has paid the full penalty for our breaking it, and has silenced its curse. His righteousness alone exceeds the righteousness of the scribes and Pharisees! Only by believing on Him can law breakers be reconciled with God.

With these general observations in mind, let us now focus on the remarkable introduction of the Sermon on the Mount. Jesus begins by describing and defining who the citizens of His kingdom are. Again, the ignorance of His audience moved Him to do so. These people had an entirely wrong perception of who the Messiah would be. They were looking for an earthly king, a Messiah who would deliver them from the bondage of the Romans. Yet Jesus had not come to deliver them from the Romans but rather to deliver His people from their sins (Matt. 1:21). He wanted to teach them immediately that His kingdom is entirely different from any earthly kingdom—it is spiritual, and its citizens have spiritual rather than political qualifications.

Jesus therefore proceeds by describing the citizens of His kingdom in a way that was so contrary to any common understanding of what constituted blessedness. These people thought, "If only I could be either a Pharisee or a scribe, I would be blessed indeed. If only I would possess great wealth, I would be blessed indeed." How many are there today who think, "If only I could have all the pleasure, all the leisure, or all the possessions I want. If only I could have power and prestige, I would be happy and blessed indeed!"

However, Jesus here tells us in dramatically different terms what real blessedness looks like. More than that, He says we cannot consider ourselves blessed or happy unless we match His description of the genuine citizens of His kingdom. In these opening verses, Christ is therefore defining for us the distinguishing traits of a true believer.

Following this chapter, we will devote a chapter to each of the first seven beatitudes. But before doing so, we will first examine the entire and composite portrait that Jesus gives us in these seven beatitudes, beginning with "Blessed are the poor" and ending with "Blessed are the peacemakers." This comprehensive portrait (Matt. 5:3–9) is followed by a description of how an ungodly world will respond to the citizens of God's spiritual kingdom. The ungodly will persecute genuine believers and will revile them and speak all manner of evil about them (Matt. 5:10–12).

Before giving you a bird's-eye perspective of the first seven beatitudes, I first wish to address their remarkable arrangement. To use a common analogy, we first need to consider what the forest looks like before examining the individual trees. A remarkable structure emerges upon examining the interrelatedness of these beatitudes. Regarding this structure, I submit that the fourth beatitude—the central beatitude of this structure—represents the heart of Christian experience. In a subsequent chapter on this beatitude, I will endeavor to supply the exegetical support for this premise.

Presently, we will therefore first briefly consider the core activity of Christian experience as expressed in verse 6: hungering and thirsting after righteousness. Second, we will consider the internal disposition of the Christian, found in verses 3 through 5, that results in this hungering and thirsting. Third, we will examine the external disposition of the Christian. He who is filled with the righteousness of which verse 6 speaks will manifest this by the fruits of his life. We will see, as Scripture says, that such will be merciful, pure in heart, and peacemakers.

Matthew 5:3–9 is the preeminent passage in all of Scripture to teach us what a Christian looks like. It is a flawless verbal portrait drawn by the Living Word Himself. It is not accidental that this portrait consists of seven components, for the biblical number seven is the number of perfection. We may therefore conclude that verses 3 through 9 set before us a perfect portrayal of every believer that ever has lived or will live until Christ returns.

Having said that, however, we need to understand that we cannot simply pick and choose the individual components of this spiritual portrait, saying, "Well, that pertains to me, and perhaps that also pertains to me." Rather, we need to understand that these seven marks are true at all times and at all seasons in the life of every believer—although not necessarily to the same extent. In some believers we see the features of this portrait more clearly than in others—just as there may be both clear and blurry photographs of a given individual. Yet, when you look at a blurry photograph, you will still be able to determine who is being depicted. This spiritual portrait thus consists of seven components that constitute an organic whole.

We also need to realize that the order in which Christ gives us the components of this portrait is not arbitrary. In other words, we cannot take these seven marks, juggle them, and then present them in just any fashion. Rather, Christ articulates these traits in a very deliberate, precise, and cumulative order: one beatitude presumes the previous one and anticipates the next.

Thus, they who are poor in spirit will mourn, they who mourn will be meek, they who exhibit all three will hunger and thirst after righteousness. Upon being filled with the righteousness they seek, they will be merciful, pure in heart, and peacemakers.

The seventh beatitude therefore most appropriately concludes in verse 9: "They shall be called the children of God." Today we would say that this is the "bottom line." Jesus is saying, "Those of whom this is true, and thus exhibit all of these marks, they, and they alone, shall be called the children of God." The Greek word rendered as "children" in verse 9 is a word that means "They shall reflect the character of God."

It is as though He is saying, "They will prove themselves to be the sons and daughters of the living God."

Let us first look at the core experiential trait of the citizens of God's kingdom, for grasping its meaning is crucial to understanding the rest. Jesus says, "Blessed [that is, supremely happy, supremely blessed] are they which do hunger and thirst after righteousness." We all understand what it means to be hungry and thirsty. Hunger and thirst are two of the most fundamental human longings, and God created us in such a way that we will be compelled to meet these basic needs. We cannot live unless those desires are met.

Jesus thus uses an analogy that is relatable to everyone. He is saying that the people of His kingdom, the children of God, will be men and women who hunger and thirst—not after physical things but rather after righteousness. In other words, a true Christian is someone who cannot be satisfied unless he obtains that righteousness for which he yearns so intensely.

What does Jesus mean by the word *righteousness*? Its literal meaning is "that which is right." God defines for us in His Word what is right and wrong. Jesus' standard of that which is right is not measured by human standards. He therefore stated, "Except your righteousness shall exceed the righteousness of the scribes and Pharisees, ye shall in no case enter into the kingdom of heaven." Therefore, righteousness is not what is right by human standards but rather what is right by God's standard.

Christians yearn for that righteousness in a twofold way: they will yearn to be in a right relationship with God and to live a life that is right—one that conforms to God's righteous standard. A true Christian cannot be satisfied unless he knows within his own soul that he is reconciled with God. However, since he loves God, he will also desire to live a right life—not to earn God's favor but rather as an expression of love for God.

Can you identify with that? This inner yearning is absolutely fundamental to true Christianity. Do you understand in some measure what it means to hunger and thirst after righteousness—that is, to yearn to be reconciled with God and to live a life that is pleasing to Him?

Jesus here brilliantly merges these two fundamental aspects of the Christian life: a yearning for *imputed* righteousness and for *imparted* righteousness. Imputed righteousness is that righteousness which God credits to my bankrupt account as a sinner—namely, the righteousness of His Son. However, we also need imparted righteousness. We need the work of the Holy Spirit enabling and equipping us to live a life that is pleasing and honoring to God. Or to put it differently, a true believer longs to be redeemed by and conformed to Christ: to be united to Him and be like Him.

That is the essence of the Christian life! To put it in theological terms, the Christian hungers and thirsts for justification and sanctification. Both of these foundational components of salvation are combined in this word *righteousness*.

And this is not something a Christian desires only once. Rather, he yearns for this his entire life. It is significant that the Beatitudes are written in the present tense, which in

Greek expresses an activity that is ongoing, continual, and/or repetitive. In these beatitudes, Jesus is therefore saying, "Blessed are they who are continually poor in spirit, who continually mourn, who are continually meek, who continually hunger and thirst after righteousness, who are continually merciful, who are continually pure in heart, and who are continually peacemakers." This is descriptive of a Christian's disposition during his entire lifetime.

The question now needs to be asked, "What produces this spiritual hunger and thirst? What causes sinners to seek righteousness?" Naturally we have no such desire. By nature we seek for our blessedness in everything other than this righteousness, and we are ignorant of our need of it. Therefore, the very first thing Jesus mentions is being poor in spirit. He says, "Blessed are they who are spiritually poor." As we will see when we examine this beatitude in depth, the poverty that Jesus describes here is a radical kind of poverty—the state of a man who literally does not have a penny in his pocket.

"Blessed are the poor in spirit." Why does Jesus begin here? He does so for the simple reason that without an experiential awareness of our spiritual poverty, we will never hunger and thirst after His righteousness. This prompted Jesus to say, "They that be whole need not a physician, but they that are sick" (Matt. 9:12). He therefore posits that blessed or happy are they who recognize their spiritual bankruptcy before God. How happy are they, indeed, because they realize that they need an alien righteousness outside of themselves—they need a savior, the Lord Jesus Christ! When the Holy Spirit works savingly in the heart, He will always begin by confronting us with our spiritual bankruptcy. If you cannot relate to that, you are missing the most foundational mark of a Christian.

Christ is saying here that this is always true—even for a man like the apostle Paul, who groaned and said, "O wretched man that I am!" (Rom. 7:24). He was deeply conscious of his spiritual poverty, which resulted in experiential mourning. As stated earlier, these beatitudes are cumulative, and this mourning represents the Christian's emotional response to his spiritual poverty. In other words, recognition of one's spiritual bankruptcy is not something that a Christian takes lightly. It causes him to grieve deeply.

Again, Christ chooses His words carefully, for the word *mourning* used here describes the grief over losing a loved one. It is reflective of a loving disposition. The reason the Christian grieves and mourns over his spiritual poverty is because the love of God has been shed abroad in his heart (Rom. 5:5). When that happens, sin becomes so ugly and vile! What a grievous matter it then will become to us that we are indeed poor in spirit! The psalmist says, "I am poor and sorrowful" (Ps. 69:29). The two are connected. Thus, there will never be such a thing as a Christian who boasts of his poverty. Rather, a true Christian grieves over it.

And that leads us to the next beatitude, "Blessed are the meek." *Meekness* is a rather difficult word to define, but you can think of it as the disposition of a person who knows his proper place before God. Thus, a Christian is humbled by his poverty of spirit, and that painful recognition will cause him to bow and surrender before God and to realize who he is in His presence.

We frequently encounter that meekness in Scripture. For example, Moses had an explosive temper, but after forty years of dwelling in the wilderness, his fiery spirit was broken. God dealt with him in such a way that he became the meekest man on earth. In Ephesians 4:1–2, the apostle Paul also speaks of that meekness: "I therefore, the prisoner of the Lord, beseech you that ye walk worthy of the vocation wherewith ye are called, with all lowliness and meekness."

Thus, a meek person is someone who sees himself as God sees him, prompting him to take his proper place before God and to humble himself in dust and ashes. A meek person recognizes the gravity of his sin and that he is deserving of God's displeasure and disfavor. We hear this meekness in the confession of David in Psalm 51:4: "Against thee, thee only, have I sinned, and done this evil in thy sight."

A recognition of one's spiritual poverty, the mourning and grieving over that poverty, and the humbling of oneself before God will culminate in a hungering and thirsting after righteousness. Such experiential awareness will cause us to realize that as spiritually bankrupt sinners, we cannot be made right with God with anything that comes from ourselves. We need a righteousness outside of ourselves. That realization will cause the Lord Jesus Christ to become, and continue to be, so very precious.

These spiritual realities are present at the beginning of one's spiritual life and will continue until death. A believer never gets beyond being a poor sinner in himself—never. As long as we live, we will mourn over sin. As long as we live, we will need to humble ourselves before God. However, that will lead us time and again to the remedy—the Lord Jesus Christ—and that will make Him increasingly precious to our souls.

All of this is implied when we say that the Holy Spirit *makes room in our hearts for Christ.* This is what it looks like! The Holy Spirit engages in this emptying work throughout the life of the believer. When a believer by renewal takes refuge to Christ, what is it that propels him to go to Him, look to Him, and rest in Him? It is the experiential realization (not just intellectual!) that he is poor in spirit, and he mourns over that. He humbles himself before God, looks outside himself, and yearns—hungers and thirsts—after the righteousness of the Lord Jesus Christ.

All who have such a hunger and thirst for righteousness will also "be filled." The word *filled* is rich indeed. Christ says that when you hunger and thirst after righteousness, your soul shall be filled to overflowing. We know that those who believe in, trust in, and are united to Christ become like Him. That affirms the genuineness of our Christianity. Our faith is not real unless in some measure we begin to resemble Him in how we think, speak, and behave. Thus, there is an inseparable connection between imputed and imparted righteousness— the righteousness that renders me acceptable to God and the righteousness by which I demonstrate that I am righteous. God's Word therefore declares that "he that doeth righteousness is righteous, even as he is righteous" (1 John 3:7).

Christ then proceeds to describe how this grace manifests itself, highlighting the essential components of a Christian life. The citizens of His kingdom are a merciful and compassionate people because they themselves are the recipients of God's mercy. When we have become acquainted with our own spiritual need, we will have a burden for the spiritual needs of others. For instance, when the Lord saves fathers or mothers, they will be burdened with the spiritual need of their children as never before. Why? Having learned what their own spiritual needs are, they now understand their children's spiritual needs. Being the recipients of mercy makes us merciful and compassionate toward others.

One striking feature of the structure of the Beatitudes is the direct parallel between the external and internal disposition of the Christian. If you were to take a sheet of paper and list the first three beatitudes on the left side, then place the fourth (hungering and thirsting after righteousness) in the middle, and finally list the last three beatitudes on the right side, doing so in parallel fashion with the first three, you would discover the obvious connection between the internal and external marks of grace: the merciful will recognize their own spiritual poverty. They will understand this experientially, and that makes them merciful and cognizant of the spiritual poverty of others.

Jesus then posits that the citizens of His kingdom are also pure in heart, thereby teaching that the moral purity of a true believer's life proceeds from within. In other words, a true Christian is not a Pharisee who cares only about keeping the outside of the cup clean. Keeping the outside pure was all that mattered to the Pharisees. Christ confronts this by teaching that the citizens of His kingdom have hearts that have been made pure by the work of the great Sanctifier and Purifier, the Holy Spirit.

Again, there is a parallel with the inner disposition of true Christians. They who mourn over sin are also pure in heart. These two marks are inseparable. We thus observe that one's inward disposition will manifest itself outwardly. Those who are pure in heart will take sin seriously, grieve over it, and yearn after holiness. A true believer is therefore not satisfied by having his act together outwardly. A true believer will wipe away many tears about matters that others will never have any knowledge of. They will grieve quietly and secretly about their sinful inclinations and desires—matters that no one will know except God. Why? Because they have been made pure in heart.

Christ also says, "My people, the citizens of my kingdom, will also be peacemakers." This is the culmination of Christ's description of the Christian, for He significantly describes the peacemakers as the children of God. What a remarkable truth this is, for, by nature, we are troublemakers! Because of our fallen nature, we are naturally inclined to hate God and our neighbor. Because of our fallen nature, our natural disposition is to live in hostility, and our world is filled with wars and rumors of war.

What a remarkable fruit of grace it is when a sinner, naturally inclined to be warlike, becomes a peacemaker! Only the transforming and renewing grace of God will produce such fruit.

Please note also that Christ does not say, "Blessed are the peace lovers." Rather, He says, "Blessed are the peacemakers." He clearly implies that God's children distinguish themselves by taking the initiative to live at peace with others. Thus, a peacemaker does not wait for the other person to make the first move; rather, he will make the first move himself.

Paul expresses this in Romans 12:18: "If it be possible, as much as lieth in you, live peaceably with all men." As Christians, we are called to do everything in our power to have harmonious relationships with our fellow men. Therefore, should any relationship not be harmonious, we must have a clear conscience that we have made a prayerful and diligent attempt to make peace. We are called to be peacemakers.

Again, there is a parallel with the inner disposition of the Christian. The meek, those who know their proper place before God, will also be peacemakers. We can readily see how the two belong together. Why are so many people troublemakers? It is because of a proud spirit. We are inclined to think too highly of ourselves and easily become offended by others. As a result, we live in discord with others.

But when we take our proper place before God, all pride and arrogance will be gone. We cannot be peacemakers unless we are willing to take the lowest place. I have a wonderful little book about living the Christian life by the German author Georg Steinberger. How striking is his opening statement: "On the cross, our Head took the lowest place, thereby giving us, His members, the lowest place. The 'brightness of [God's] glory' (Heb. 1:3) became 'despised and rejected of men' (Isa. 53:3). Since then we have but *one* right,

namely, to be the lowest and the least. If we believe ourselves
to be worthy of more, we have not yet understood the cross."[1]
Think about that!

Peacemakers are willing to take the lowest place. Years
ago, a godly man taught me an unforgettable lesson. He said,
"When you are involved in conflict, the best way to resolve it
is to act as if you are 99 percent at fault and the other person
is 1 percent—even if in reality it is the other way around.
Take the lowest place."

"Blessed are the peacemakers: for they shall be called the
children of God." The apostle articulates this in Hebrews
12:14: "Follow peace with all men." Paul speaks the same
language: "God hath called us to peace" (1 Cor. 7:15) and "Be
of one mind, live in peace; and the God of love and peace
shall be with you" (2 Cor. 13:11).

Since God Himself is the great Peacemaker, Jesus is saying, "They who are peacemakers manifest something of the
character of their heavenly Father." Peacemakers resemble
their Father, the great Peacemaker, who sent His Son into
the world to bring peace on earth. Rather than waiting in
vain for us to take the initiative, He took the initiative by
sending His Son to reconcile sinners unto Himself. This

---

1. Georg Steinberger, *Kleine Lichter auf den Weg der Nachfolge* (Stuttgart, Germany: Christliches Verlagshaus, GMBH, 1986), 5. The original
text: "Am Kreuz hat unser Haupt den untersten Platz eingenommen und
hat auch uns, Seinen Gliedern, den untersten Platz gegeben. Der 'Abglanz
des unsichtbaren Gottes' (Heb. 1:3) wurde der 'Allerverachteste' (Jes.
53:3). Seitdem haben wir nur *ein* Recht, nämlich der Unterste und Letzte
zu sein. Wenn wir auf etwas mehr Anspruch machen, haben wir noch
nicht das Kreuz verstanden."

prompted the angels to sing in the fields of Ephrata, "Glory to God in the highest, and on earth peace, good will toward men" (Luke 2:14).

In summary, God's children will have an internal disposition of being poor in spirit, mournful, and meek, causing them to hunger and thirst after righteousness. Then the righteousness for which they yearn will spill over into their lives and cause them to be merciful, pure of heart and life, and peacemakers.

The manifestation of such fruits will provoke an ungodly world to hate us. The world has no problem with nominal Christianity, but it is offended by true Christianity. Therefore, in this eighth and final beatitude, Jesus also pronounces as blessed "they which are persecuted for righteousness' sake." True Christians do not seek to provoke the world, but their genuine godliness provokes the ungodly, who would love to eliminate such Christianity. Jesus tells the children of God that a hostile world will say "all manner of evil against you falsely, for my sake." But He then adds, "Rejoice, and be exceeding glad: for great is your reward in heaven: for so persecuted they the prophets which were before you" (Matt. 5:10–12).

Thus, we have attempted to give you a global overview of Christ's portrait of the Christian. We have taken a look at the whole forest before examining the individual trees in the chapters that follow. In the Beatitudes, Christ defines true blessedness. Only in proportion to our experience of these beatitudes will we experience biblical happiness or blessedness. The opposite is also true! Cursed are they who are not poor in spirit, who do not mourn over their sins, and who are not meek. Cursed are they who do not hunger and thirst after righteousness. Cursed are they who are not merciful, who are not pure in heart, and who are not peacemakers.

To which category do you belong? There is no other alternative! Do you recognize yourself in the portrait of the Beatitudes? Do they in some measure describe your inner disposition, your soul's yearning, and your walk of life? If you do not recognize yourself at all in this portrait of true spirituality, you do not yet belong to God's kingdom. You need to take refuge in the Christ who has provided us with this portrait. You need to cry out that He would instruct you by His Spirit, so that the distinguishing marks of the Beatitudes will also become an experiential reality for you.

Discussion Questions

1. Why is it important to recognize that Christ's objective in preaching the Sermon on the Mount was not merely to instruct His audience regarding the essentials of biblical morality?

2. Why would it have been such a stunning statement to His audience when Christ declared that unless their righteousness exceeded that of the scribes and Pharisees they could not enter the kingdom of heaven?

3. Why did Christ confront His audience with the spirituality of the law rather than the letter of the law?

4. What important conclusion can we draw from the fact that Christ's spiritual portrait consists of seven components?

5. How does the second half of the seventh beatitude, "They shall be called the children of God," apply to all seven beatitudes?

6. What is meant by the statement that in the Beatitudes Christ gives us an "all or nothing" description of the Christian?

7. Why is it significant that Christ uses the present tense in each beatitude?

8. How do the first three beatitudes describe the Holy Spirit's work to make (and continue to make) room in the heart for Christ and His righteousness?

9. What is the important parallel between the inner disposition of the Christian (beatitudes 1–3) and the external disposition of the Christian (beatitudes 5–7)?

10. What marks the blessedness of those for whom the Beatitudes are an experiential reality?

Chapter 1

THE POOR IN SPIRIT

Blessed are the poor in spirit:
for theirs is the kingdom of heaven.
—MATTHEW 5:3

If you were to search the Scriptures for the word *blessed*, you would discover that the majority of occurrences are in the Old Testament. Not surprisingly, therefore, the Beatitudes found at the commencement of Jesus' Sermon on the Mount are all rooted in the Old Testament Scriptures. His objective in preaching this sermon was to expound the foundational truths of the Old Testament. After all, it was the Bible of the church of Israel. Christ therefore preached from these Scriptures and quoted them regularly. The Old Testament contained the entire body of truth, which Jesus Himself had come to fulfill.

However, the interpretation of the Old Testament Scriptures had been grievously corrupted by the scribes and Pharisees. Because of their erroneous teaching, the majority of Israel's population lived in spiritual ignorance about the coming Messiah. Since these misguided souls had entirely wrong ideas regarding the kingdom of God, their understanding of what it meant to be a citizen of that kingdom was also erroneous. The Lord Jesus therefore began His sermon by painting for us a verbal portrait of what a Christian—a citizen of God's kingdom—looks like.

In the previous chapter we saw that each of the first seven beatitudes is a feature of that portrait. As is true of any portrait, this spiritual portrait can be assessed accurately only when one looks at all the features simultaneously. To facilitate viewing the whole portrait as an organic entity, we have therefore first given a wide-angle view of the entire picture, showing us the interconnectedness of its individual traits.

All the traits articulated in the Beatitudes will be found in some measure in the lives of all genuine Christians, albeit not equally. Although there are weak and strong Christians, the first seven beatitudes constitute an integrated whole, and therefore you cannot arbitrarily select which of these applies to you. As we will see, one beatitude presumes the previous one and anticipates the next. In the next chapter, we will focus on the blessedness of those who mourn, which presupposes that the one who mourns does so because he knows himself to be poor in spirit.

Let us thus begin by examining the first of these beatitudes—namely, being poor in spirit. We will first examine what Jesus means when He describes believers as being poor in spirit. Christ does not merely say, "Blessed are the poor"; rather, He explicitly says, "Blessed are the poor *in spirit*." Second, we will address the happiness of the people who embody this beatitude. At first glance, the dispositions of being poor in spirit and happy appear to be mutually exclusive. We will therefore discuss why Jesus pronounces the poor in spirit to be happy as well as what that happiness consists of. And third, we will consider the citizenship of the poor in spirit, for Jesus remarkably says that they are citizens of His kingdom.

The Poverty of the Poor in Spirit

Jesus' audience was astonished by His preaching, which was so different from what they were accustomed to hearing from the scribes and Pharisees. The gist of their teaching would have been "Blessed are they who are like us; blessed are they who are as prominent as we are; blessed are they who know as much as we do; blessed are they who are as righteous as we are." But Jesus begins His sermon by saying, "Blessed are the poor in spirit"; that is, blessed are they who consciously recognize their spiritual poverty.

Jesus never used words randomly. There are two Greek words that can be translated as "poor." One refers to people who are poor in a general sense. They live under very humble circumstances, have very little income, have no money in the bank, barely make ends meet, and live from day to day. Although poor in a general sense, they are not utterly destitute. The other Greek word describes someone who has been reduced to beggary, has literally nothing but the clothes on his back, does not have a penny to his name, is radically poor, and is thus utterly bankrupt or destitute. Jesus chooses the latter word, thereby declaring that the poor in spirit realize how spiritually destitute they are, recognize before God that they are utterly void of all righteousness, and recognize that they are spiritually poor in the most radical sense.

Such is Christ's assessment of our state as fallen sons and daughters of Adam! We are by nature spiritually destitute and bankrupt—a condition we are utterly unaware of without divine illumination. We are as oblivious to our desperate plight as the woman who met Jesus at a well in Samaria (John 4). She was entirely ignorant of her condition until Jesus exposed her spiritual bankruptcy and poverty. Our natural condition is like hers.

Why is our spiritual poverty so radical? We can answer that question correctly only when we reflect on man's state prior to his tragic fall in Paradise. Neither the gospel nor the objective of God's redeeming work will be evident to us unless we reference it against the background of man's original creation. God's goal in redemption is to restore fallen man to what He originally created him to be.

By highlighting this radical poverty of spirit, Christ implies that man in his original state was unspeakably rich. What constituted these riches? What made Adam and Eve so unspeakably wealthy? As the crown jewels of His creation, Adam and Eve were created in the image of God's only begotten Son. As His created son and daughter, they reflected the glory of His eternal Son, and were also temples of His Holy Spirit. God therefore uniquely crafted Adam and Eve out of the dust of the earth, molding and building them to be a temple for Himself. Upon finishing His masterpiece, He breathed His Spirit into them, and they became temples of the Holy Ghost.

Thus, before they fell, Adam and Eve were truly Spirit-filled people. They were unspeakably rich because God created them explicitly to be the dwelling place of His own Spirit. God Himself dwelt in Adam and Eve! Prior to their fall, they were God-focused, God-centered, and God-oriented. But the moment they rebelled, God withdrew His Spirit from them, and instead of being temples of the Holy Ghost they became the synagogues of Satan. When God withdrew Himself, they became poor in spirit, for that which once fulfilled their lives and gave them purpose was now absent.

Consequently, Adam and Eve did not merely lose Paradise and eternal life when they fell—they lost God Himself! Having been created to find our purpose and fulfillment in the God who created us, we lost everything when we fell in Adam, for we lost God Himself! As fallen sinners, our spiritual bankruptcy is thus defined by the fact that our lives are empty and we are naturally devoid of the Spirit of God.

Reader, if God is not yet your portion, your life is empty. You may think otherwise, because as human beings we do everything we can to fill that void with something other than God. Yet since our hearts were created to be filled with God, nothing can ultimately satisfy us but God Himself. If, therefore, God is not your heavenly Father in Christ, your life is void of true meaning, and everything you enjoy in this life is but an empty substitute for what really ought to fill your heart.

In this opening beatitude, Jesus says that those who become experientially aware of that reality are blessed. Blessed are they who have become conscious of that profoundly troubling truth—who begin to understand their spiritual poverty and what it means to be a sinner. Blessed are they who are illuminated by the Spirit to discover that they are without God and therefore without hope in the world (Eph. 2:12).

The Blessedness of the Poor in Spirit

This initial, growing, and continued awareness of our spiritual bankruptcy is the pathway whereby the Holy Spirit leads us to experience the unsearchable riches found in Christ. Jesus teaches us in this opening beatitude that the abiding awareness of our radical spiritual poverty is foundational to the Christian life. Without that experiential awareness of one's spiritual bankruptcy, a person cannot be a citizen of God's kingdom. Without that awareness, we will never desire the salvation that God has provided in His only begotten Son; we will never yearn for the Lord Jesus Christ; we will never hunger and thirst after Him and His righteousness; we will see no beauty in Jesus that we should desire Him (Isa. 53:2).

Unbelievers continue to live daily without Christ, for they neither see nor feel their need of Him as a savior from sin. If you are one who continues to be oblivious to that reality, you are wretched indeed, for you do not see your need for Christ. As long as you do not see your need of Him, and thus do not believe in Him, you are hell-bound. Jesus teaches that very plainly, for by pronouncing the poor in spirit to be blessed, He implies that all who are still oblivious of their spiritual poverty are accursed of God.

The Holy Spirit's work, however, is to make room in our hearts for Christ by confronting us with our spiritual bankruptcy, teaching us that we are radically poor and that there is nothing in us that can render us acceptable to God. What a painful discovery that is! That discovery caused the publican to stay in the back of the temple. He was painfully aware of his spiritual poverty, and groaned, "God be merciful to me a sinner." In the front of the temple stood a Pharisee, boasting of who he was and thanking God that he was not like that publican. Sadly, this proud man was ignorant of his spiritual poverty.

Let me emphasize again what was stated earlier: the awareness of one's spiritual poverty is not something a person experiences only at the beginning of his spiritual life. The Beatitudes are in the present tense, and Jesus is thereby saying that these traits are always characteristic of the citizens of His kingdom. The people of God will always be a people who are experientially and painfully aware that they are poor in spirit.

Thus, an unmistakable trait of true spirituality will be humility, for nothing is as humbling as being aware of who we really are before God. When the Spirit of God opens our eyes, we begin to see ourselves as God sees us. The difference between the publican and the Pharisee is that the Pharisee compared himself to others. When he did so, he came out on top. But the publican saw himself as God sees us, causing him to bow his head and smite his breast, saying, "God be merciful to me a sinner."

As long as the Christian lives, he will never get beyond that painful awareness of his spiritual poverty. In fact, that awareness will increase because in order to grow in grace, we must also grow in the experiential knowledge of our radical bankruptcy. The more we realize how deeply destitute we are, the more precious Jesus will become to us and the more we will trust in Him alone. We will then increasingly understand what Paul meant when he said, "Christ is all, and in all" (Col. 3:11). And so it is! Christ will be all and in all only for a people who have nothing at all. Blessed indeed are the poor in spirit, for they will continually look outside of themselves to the Lord Jesus Christ and His finished work!

How painful it is for believers when they think they are making some progress in the way of holiness and sanctification, only to be confronted again with the radical nature of their remaining and indwelling sin. God, in His fatherly wisdom, will at times even permit them to stumble as a way of reminding them who they remain in themselves. In this foundational beatitude, Jesus says that it is a blessing when that happens—when once again we fall flat on our faces, so to speak. It is a blessing when we realize afresh how spiritually poor we are and remain, for it will prompt us to look outside of ourselves to Christ and boast in Him alone.

The apostle Paul never got beyond this. Although he was a man who knew more of Christ than any man has ever known, he could only say of himself, "For I know that in me (that is, in my flesh,) dwelleth no good thing: for to will is present with me; but how to perform that which is good I find not…. O wretched man that I am! who shall deliver me from the body of this death?" (Rom. 7:18, 24).

However, it was precisely that painful and experiential awareness that also caused him to cry out with holy joy, "I thank God through Jesus Christ our Lord!" He knew that in Christ there was deliverance even for a wretched man, as he knew himself to be. Thus, Jesus says that they who discover—and continue to discover—their spiritual poverty are happy and blessed indeed! The experiential realization of one's sinfulness is the pathway to true happiness and joy, for it is the pathway that leads us to Christ, in whom alone we can find salvation and reconciliation with God.

To men and women of the world it seems absurd to say, "Happy are the poor in spirit, happy are they that mourn, and happy are the meek." This is totally contrary to the world's thinking. It seems like such a paradox, for Jesus is saying that they who become and remain supremely unhappy with themselves are actually supremely blessed.

In the song of Hannah (1 Sam. 2), Hannah makes a remarkable observation, saying, "The LORD maketh poor, and maketh rich: he bringeth low, and lifteth up" (v. 7). In short, He does both! In Psalm 68:10, we read, "Thou, O God, hast prepared of thy goodness for the poor," and in Psalm 132:15, "I will abundantly bless her provision: I will satisfy her poor with bread." This is a reference to the Bread of Life, the Lord Jesus Christ. To put it simply, if you have never experienced how bankrupt you are before God, you also will not know the Lord Jesus Christ experientially. Christ is telling us plainly that knowing one's spiritual bankruptcy is the foundation of all true experience. All other graces are built on that foundation. Salvation will never be experienced without the experiential knowledge of one's spiritual poverty.

By continually making us aware of our spiritual bankruptcy, the Spirit of God teaches us that being fruitful believers means that one will not only initially and repeatedly take refuge to Christ but will also abide in Him. In John 15:5, Jesus says, "I am the vine, ye are the branches: He that abideth in me, and I in him, the same bringeth forth much fruit: for without me ye can do nothing." Hence, without Him and apart from abiding in Him, one cannot be spiritually fruitful.

The ongoing ministry of God's Spirit is needed to make us realize that we cannot progress in the Christian life apart from Christ—without fleeing to Him, trusting in Him, leaning on Him, and abiding in Him. That experiential awareness, as painful as it may be, will be profitable to our souls, for it will lead us to Christ. The Spirit will always lead us to Christ, for it is His great work to glorify Christ by leading poor and bankrupt sinners to embrace Him by faith.

Blessed are those who see themselves as God sees them—who are so conscious of their spiritual poverty that they lose all hope in themselves and of contributing anything to their salvation! How blessed are they indeed who come to that realization and trust in Christ alone!

That such poor and bankrupt sinners are called blessed is such an astonishing and humbling truth for believers who understand experientially that they were deserving of being accursed of God because of their sin! What does it mean to be accursed? It means that the execution of God's wrath due to our sin is inescapable. As long as God's curse rests on us, we cannot escape the execution of His wrath. And the Bible says, "Cursed is every one that continueth not in all things which are written in the book of the law to do them" (Gal. 3:10). Consequently, if we transgress God's law, even only one commandment, we are subject to the inescapable curse of the law.

How can Jesus say that such spiritually bankrupt sinners are blessed? The cross of Calvary, and the Savior nailed to that cross, provides us with the answer. Jesus died neither by the sword nor by beheading; rather, He was crucified because He, as the divinely appointed Substitute, was made a curse in our place. Paul tells us in Galatians 3:13, "Christ hath redeemed us from the curse of the law, being made a curse for us." Christ, the Lawgiver, willingly subjected Himself to the curse of His own law—not only identifying Himself with that curse but becoming the embodiment of it! In so doing, He merited an everlasting blessing for fallen sons and daughters of Adam worthy of God's everlasting curse.

What a glorious truth indeed! Because Jesus was made a curse, God can now bless the poor in spirit—guilty, bankrupt, and wretched sinners! Jesus knew that when He uttered the words on the cross, "Father, forgive them; for they know not what they do" (Luke 23:34), the only way such sinners could be called blessed was by Him being made a curse for them on the cross of Calvary. He knew this was the only way in which these beatitudes could become a blessed reality in the lives of the spiritual citizens of His kingdom.

The Citizenship of the Poor in Spirit

Christ concludes this beatitude with an extraordinary statement: the kingdom of heaven belongs to these poor, needy sinners whom He declares blessed! Life doesn't get better than that, because to be part of that kingdom is everything. It means that we belong to God's people, who will receive all the blessings of that kingdom—both now and forever. The citizens of that kingdom enjoy the favor of the King of kings.

However, without the experiential recognition of one's spiritual poverty, one will never be a true believer in Christ—nor a citizen of Christ's kingdom. The citizens of that spiritual kingdom, the poor in spirit, shall willingly surrender themselves to the kingship of Jesus. This is precisely what you and I refuse to do by nature. As sinners by birth and by practice, we live in rebellion toward God and are not citizens of His moral kingdom. Dear reader, are you still an unbeliever today? Are you still not earnestly seeking after God? Then you are still living a life of rebellion toward Him.

That will change only when you become experientially aware of who you are in God's sight. That awareness will humble you greatly. The discovery and recognition of our profound spiritual poverty cannot but produce the fruit of humility. Thus, in this opening beatitude, Christ posits that such Spirit-wrought humility is an entrance requirement into God's kingdom.

By nature we do not believe we are poor in spirit—we think we are rich and have no need of anything, as Revelation 3:17 clarifies: "Because thou sayest, I am rich, and increased with goods, and have need of nothing; and knowest not that thou art wretched, and miserable, and poor, and blind, and naked."

Like the Pharisees, we think highly of ourselves, even though we may talk like a poor sinner. Let me illustrate. A woman once came to her pastor, wanting to impress him with her humility and spirituality. Seeking to portray a very humble demeanor, she said, "Oh pastor, I am such an awful sinner." He immediately replied, "Yes, that's what I have heard about you." She then rose up in anger and said, "What did they tell you about me?" Her angry response revealed that her humility was obviously not genuine. Even though she talked as one poor in spirit, in reality she thought very highly of herself. Had she truly been poor in spirit, she would have responded that matters were worse than her pastor suspected.

Being poor in spirit will therefore never be the natural disposition of fallen sinners. Pride is the natural bent of our fallen natures. It is the worship of self—the wretched inclination of sinners who still believe Satan's original lie that we shall be as God. Our sinful pride therefore needs to be broken, and the Spirit of God knows how to break that pride. As a result of His supernatural and transforming work, He will cause us to acknowledge before God who we really are in His sight. That will humble us greatly!

Therefore, we know that David was a regenerated man by his response to Nathan's convicting message that he was guilty of fornication, deceit, and murder. If there had been no grace in David's heart, Nathan would have died on the spot. But David knew himself to be a poor sinner, and he bowed his head and humbled himself before God. We need to understand that one cannot be a citizen of the kingdom of heaven with a proud spirit. Only those who experientially know themselves to be poor in spirit, and who seek salvation outside of themselves in Christ, will prove themselves to be genuine citizens of the kingdom of God.

The spiritual key of the gospel opens the kingdom to those who trust in Christ by faith. Only sinners who are experientially poor in spirit will, by faith, flee to Him and trust in Him. The world would say, "In order to be part of a kingdom, to be part of an elite club, you need to have qualifying credentials." Jesus, however, says that the one essential credential for being a citizen of His kingdom is that you must be poor in spirit—then the kingdom of heaven is yours. Note that He doesn't say "shall be yours" but rather "is yours." If, by the grace of God, we have truly acknowledged and endorsed our spiritual poverty, Christ is saying, reverently speaking, "Sinner, I can now welcome you into My kingdom. There is room in My kingdom for the poor in spirit."

How rich is the promise Jesus attaches to His pronouncement that the poor in spirit are blessed! When He says that yours is the kingdom of heaven, He is saying that this is a privilege that will never be revoked. It will endure forever. In her song, Hannah says, "He raiseth up the poor out of the dust, and lifteth up the beggar from the dunghill, to set them among princes, and to make them inherit the throne of glory" (1 Sam. 2:8). Notice how the first beatitude is rooted in the Old Testament. This passage was Hannah's way of saying "Blessed are the poor in spirit." She calls them the poor and the beggar from the dunghill who will be set among princes and inherit the throne of glory.

And so, dear reader, do you belong to the poor in spirit? Is that a proper description of who you are? Do the words of the first beatitude resonate with you? Can you identify with them? Have you been taught by God's Spirit how spiritually bankrupt and sinful you are? Do you perceive experientially how corrupt, vile, and unworthy you are? Has that caused you to look outside of yourself to the Lord Jesus Christ, who is such a profoundly suitable savior for such a sinner as you are?

The Puritan Thomas Watson makes the following remarkable observation in his famous sermons on the Beatitudes: "This is the difference between a hypocrite and a child of God: the hypocrite is ever telling what he has. A child of God complains of what he lacks."[1] Watson is simply saying that the counterfeit believer will view himself as an accomplished Christian, whereas the genuine believer will readily admit how deficient he is and remains, and that he has but a small beginning of new obedience in Christ.

Reader, if you have not become experientially aware that you are poor in spirit, you are cursed rather than blessed. As stated earlier, every beatitude implies a curse. Thus, cursed are those who are not poor in spirit, who do not mourn, who are not meek, who do not hunger and thirst after righteousness.

---

1. Thomas Watson, *The Beatitudes* (Edinburgh: Banner of Truth, 1975), 46.

We are either believers or unbelievers; we are either citizens of God's kingdom or we are not. What is your identity?

But thanks be to God, in the gospel Christ sets before you an open door into His everlasting kingdom. He is saying, "I am the door: by me if any man enter in, he shall be saved" (John 10:9). Therefore, if you are compelled to confess that you are not yet a citizen of that kingdom, cast yourself at the feet of Jesus, the complete Savior for completely lost sinners. Only in Him will you find the righteousness that exceeds the righteousness of the scribes and Pharisees—a righteousness offered freely to poor, bankrupt, corrupt, guilty, and hell-worthy sinners. We have the precious promise of His Word that such sinners who come to Him shall in no wise be cast out (John 6:37).

And dear believer, even though the reoccurring awareness of your spiritual poverty can be so painful and unsettling, Jesus says to you, "Fear not, little flock; for it is your Father's good pleasure to give you the kingdom" (Luke 12:32). One day you will discover as never before what it means to be in Christ, and you will then hear out of His mouth, "Come, ye blessed of my Father, inherit the kingdom prepared for you from the foundation of the world" (Matt. 25:34).

Discussion Questions

1. In describing spiritual poverty, why is it significant that Christ uses a word that refers to radical poverty rather than merely a generic poverty?

2. What constitutes the essence of our spiritual poverty?

3. Why is the experiential awareness of one's spiritual poverty so foundational for the experience of the Christian?

4. Why do God's children, in this life, never progress beyond being poor in spirit?

5. How do the Beatitudes clearly teach us that the experiential awareness of spiritual poverty will never be a stand-alone experience?

6. Why is the awareness of one's spiritual poverty also essential for the life of sanctification?

7. What connection is there between being poor in spirit and growing "in grace, and in the knowledge of our Lord and Saviour Jesus Christ" (2 Peter 3:18)?

8. What is meant by the expression "The King became a beggar so that beggars might become kings"?

9. Explain Thomas Watson's pithy remark: "The hypocrite is ever telling what he has. A child of God complains of what he lacks."

Chapter 2

SPIRITUAL MOURNERS COMFORTED

Blessed are they that mourn:
for they shall be comforted.
—MATTHEW 5:4

Having established the awareness of one's spiritual poverty as the foundational experience of the citizens of God's kingdom, Christ continues His description of these citizens as "they that mourn." This too is one of the essential features of Christ's verbal portrait of the Christian. We will examine this feature by considering the nature of this mourning, its blessedness, and the comfort that is promised to such mourners.

The Nature of This Mourning

The mourning of which Jesus speaks is not natural mourning. Christ is not calling blessed those who are merely grieving because of circumstances pertaining to this life. This mistaken assumption is often expressed on sympathy cards. This beatitude does not address the mourning that is natural to all sinful men as they must deal with the inescapable reality of sorrow and death in a fallen world. In fact, the traits articulated in the Beatitudes are not descriptive of traits that might naturally be found in men. All of these marks are spiritual—the result of the Holy Spirit's work within the heart.

Thus, Christ addresses a mourning that is intimately related to the poverty of spirit delineated in the previous beatitude. He is saying that His people, in recognizing who they are before God, will mourn over their spiritual bankruptcy. And why do true believers grieve over their spiritual poverty? Why will true believers not speak of it casually and on a merely intellectually level? Why is their experiential awareness of this poverty so deeply painful to them that it will cause them to mourn?

The meaning of the term *to mourn* will provide us with the answer. As the Living Word of God, Christ chose His words carefully and precisely. The word He uses here to describe the mourning of the poor in spirit is analogous to the mourning of someone who has lost a loved one. What characterizes the mourning of someone who has to bury his or her beloved spouse, of children burying their parents, or of parents burying children? It is an expression of love for the one who died.

The explicit mourning of this beatitude is thus a mourning that proceeds from and is defined by love. It is the spiritual mourning of a regenerated heart. In regeneration, the Holy Spirit makes a sinner spiritually alive, making him a new creation. The moment the Spirit grants life to a sinner dead in trespasses and sins (Eph. 2:1), the heart will be kindled with love for God. With that love being shed abroad in his heart

(Rom. 5:5), the regenerated sinner will begin to love God and everything that pertains to Him: His Word, His law, His church, His house, His service, His Son, and so on. He will then recognize and begin to love the law as the will of God, which in turn will produce heartfelt spiritual mourning, for he will then begin to grasp that his spiritual poverty—his comprehensive and systemic sinfulness—is defined by his transgression of the law and his failure to obey it.

Psalm 51 articulates this spiritual mourning for us, for even though David had sinned grievously, he was and remained a man who deeply loved God. He had sinned heinously and grievously, living without real repentance for at least nine months. In response to Nathan's withering indictment, however, David bowed his head and mourned deeply. As a spiritual mourner, he confessed, "Wash me thoroughly from mine iniquity, and cleanse me from my sin. For I acknowledge my transgressions: and my sin is ever before me. Against thee, thee only, have I sinned, and done this evil in thy sight" (Ps. 51:2–4).

Such a confession is the hallmark of God's saving work in the heart. He repeatedly awakens sinners to the reality that they are transgressors, and that becomes a matter of great and abiding sorrow to regenerated souls. Thus, a true believer is someone who will grieve over sin until his last breath. The prophet Zechariah prophesied that, when the Spirit would be poured out on the people of Israel and they would be convicted of having crucified the Messiah, "they shall look upon me whom they have pierced, and they shall mourn for him, as one mourneth for his only son, and shall be in bitterness for him, as one that is in bitterness for his first-born" (Zech. 12:10).

There you have it: mourning as an expression of love! Such mourning is a foundational trait of genuine spiritual life. In fact, Jesus teaches unequivocally that in this world the true citizens of His kingdom will always grieve over sin.

Do you recognize yourself in that? Are you one of those mourners in Zion? Have you ever grieved over your sinner-ship before God? Do you understand what David meant when he said, "Against thee, thee only, have I sinned, and done this evil in thy sight"? Reader, if you cannot at all relate to such mourning, you are not a Christian and do not belong to God's kingdom. We live in a day when many claim to be Christians who know nothing of such mourning—many who embrace a Christianity that one might refer to as a frivo-lous Christianity. It is defined by false happiness, and there is a complete absence of such spiritual mourning.

However, Jesus also does not say, "Blessed are they who produce a flood of tears; blessed are they who weep loudly." Rather, He is describing here a state of the heart. We all have a unique constitution, causing some believers to respond to the bitter reality of their sinnership more emotionally than others. Thus, Jesus is not saying that physical tears deter-mine whether you belong to His kingdom. Instead He is speaking of a state of the heart and a continual experiential awareness of who we are and remain in ourselves. A true believer is indwelt by the Holy Spirit, who actively and con-tinually teaches us and will always keep us conscious of our sinnership—of our inherent unholiness.

True believers will thus mourn continually over their transgressions and indwelling corruption until God delivers them from the body of this death. Think only of all the sins you have committed in thought, word, and deed during this past week. How painful can be the spiritual and experiential awareness of having sinned against God and each other! At such moments we can be so vulnerable to the whisperings of Satan, saying, "You say that you're a Christian. Aren't you fooling yourself? Do you think that a true believer would have thought, said, or done such a thing? Do you think a true believer would have so readily yielded to that kind of temptation?" How devious is the liar from the beginning! First he will endeavor to make us fall into sin, and then, when we have sinned, he will seek to bring us to despair by blinding us to the gospel and its comfort.

A true believer will be painfully aware of the fountain of corruption that abides within him. True believers will therefore mourn before God over those sinful thoughts and inclinations that others know nothing about. They will be conscious of the fact that God knows their hearts and the secrets within. They live in *coram Deo*, "in the presence of God." Thus, when a sinful thought crosses a believer's mind or when he senses a sinful desire, he will grieve over it and confess it before God. Here the difference between the believer and a hypocrite becomes apparent. The hypocrite is concerned only about the outside of the cup. As long as the external and visible aspect of his life is acceptable, he is not concerned about what transpires within.

It is not so with a true believer! He can understand David, who said in Psalm 38:6–7, "I go mourning all the day long. For my loins are filled with a loathsome disease." Dear reader, are you experientially acquainted with that loathsome disease?

One of the marks of spiritual growth is an ever deepening awareness of that loathsomeness that causes believers to mourn. They mourn over their lack of conformity to Christ. They know they are called to a life of Christlike obedience. Yet so often they perceive so little Christlikeness within themselves. Believers also mourn over their wretched tendency toward unbelief that discredits God and the promises of the gospel. Despite all that God has done for us, and that He has never proven Himself to be unfaithful, we so readily default to unbelief. Immediately following Hebrews 11, the renowned chapter on faith, the apostle addresses unbelief as being the sin that so easily besets us.

Believers also mourn over not having an experiential sense of God's favor or nearness. Sometimes God can seem so distant that believers may think, "Has God forgotten me?" How painful that can be! To a believer there is nothing sweeter than to experience a sense of God's favor and nearness. When that is absent, he will grieve over it—especially when he senses that it is sin that causes separation between God and his soul. Romans 7 is therefore so highly valued by all believers, for there we hear the groaning of the apostle Paul, an experienced and mature Christian, who mourns deeply over his sinfulness and indwelling corruption, exclaiming in holy despair, "O wretched man that I am!"

The Blessedness of Mourning

However, as deeply as Paul mourned, he greatly rejoices when immediately thereafter he cries out, "I thank God through Jesus Christ our Lord." This profoundly illustrates why Jesus says, "Blessed are they that mourn"—who grieve over sin, over their indwelling corruption, and over the loss of God's nearness and favor. He proceeds to define the blessedness of all for whom this is a painful reality, adding, "for they shall be comforted."

Believers do mourn indeed, but they will also be comforted! The Greek verb "to comfort" is *parakaleo*, and its noun form is *parakletos*. We recognize this noun at once as one of the glorious titles of the Holy Spirit (Paraclete). Jesus said, "If I go not away, the Comforter will not come unto you" (John 16:7). Here Christ refers to His own Spirit as the Comforter, for it is the special and prominent ministry of the Holy Spirit to comfort the mourners in Zion.

To understand the Spirit's ministry as the Comforter, we need to reflect for a moment on His unique place in the Trinity and His work in the divine economy of redemption. Scripture identifies the Holy Spirit as both the Spirit of the Father and the Spirit of the Son (Rom. 8:9). Scripture also records for us that the Holy Spirit proceeds from both the Father and the Son (John 15:26; 16:7). That double procession is *the* unique distinctive of the Holy Spirit as the third person in the divine Trinity. His procession gives us a glimpse into the fact that the Trinity is an everlasting love relationship between the Father and the Son, who dwell in constant and infinite fellowship with each other in the person of the Holy Spirit. In His glorious person, He is the personal bond of love that unites the Father and the Son. Thus, in the Spirit, the Father communicates His infinite love to His Son (the Spirit proceeding from the Father to the Son), and in the Spirit, the Son communicates His infinite love to the Father (the Spirit proceeding from the Son to the Father).

The Spirit's ontological function within the Trinity also defines the nature of His redeeming work in the hearts of sinners. As the Spirit of the Father, He will infallibly lead us to the Son. Thus, when He convicts us of our sin, He is doing so in order to lead us to the Son, the Lord Jesus Christ, to find salvation and comfort in Him alone. Jesus therefore said, "Howbeit when he, the Spirit of truth, is come, he will guide you into all truth.... He shall glorify me: for he shall receive of mine, and shall shew it unto you" (John 16:13–14). As the Spirit of the Father, He will glorify the Son and lead sinners to Him. Only in the Son, as the Mediator Jesus Christ, can we be reconciled with the Father and receive a full pardon for our sins.

This explains why Christ designates the Holy Spirit as the Comforter, for He will see to it that sinners cannot find any comfort outside of the Lord Jesus Christ. He will not permit us to find comfort in our mourning, our tears, our repentance, or our conversion—as precious as these spiritual fruits are—because the Holy Spirit will not rest until we rest in Jesus alone.

In fact, the Holy Spirit engages Himself as such during the entire lifetime of believers, continually and repeatedly making room for the Lord Jesus Christ in our soul. In so doing, He will make Christ increasingly precious to us. There can be no spiritual growth without this spiritual mourning and growing awareness of our sinful condition. Only in this way will we grow in grace and in the knowledge of the Lord Jesus Christ, not having any expectation of self. Only then will Christ become and remain the sole resting place for our soul, increasingly becoming our all and in all.

The Comfort Promised to the Mourners in Zion

Therefore, the Spirit will never do a half work! When He causes us to mourn, He also comforts us, for in the way of mourning over our spiritual poverty He makes room in our hearts for Jesus and His finished work. The Holy Spirit will empty us in order to fill us with the blessed fullness found in Jesus Christ.

However, the Spirit of the Father who leads us to the Son will also, as the Spirit of the Son, lead us to the Father. The ultimate objective of redemption is that in obtaining full reconciliation in the Son, one may return and be restored into the favor of the Father. The definitive outcome of the redeeming work of a triune God will be the restoration of the Father-child relationship between God and fallen sons and daughters of Adam. That's what Adam enjoyed and then lost!

Jesus has this in mind when He says, "Blessed are the poor in spirit." The essence of our spiritual poverty and wretchedness is rooted in the fact that, in Adam, we have lost that Father-child relationship with God. Thus, if God is not your Father, then all that you may have enjoyed in this world is but imaginary happiness. It is counterfeit and illusory, for in the end you will have nothing. If God is not your heavenly Father in Christ, you are truly of all men most miserable! If, however, God is your Father in Christ, you have everything indeed (1 Cor. 3:22–23)!

Therefore, the same Spirit who leads us to the Son will also lead us to the Father. He first leads us to the Son to find forgiveness and reconciliation in Christ, then He leads us to the Father. On the basis of the finished work of Christ, we may then rejoice in the fact that God shall forever be our Father. Jesus profoundly summarized this by saying to Mary Magdalene on the day of His resurrection, "Go to my brethren, and say unto them, I ascend unto my Father, and your Father; and to my God, and your God" (John 20:17). To put it plainly, Christ is saying that the purpose of His redeeming work—His death and resurrection—is that His Father can be our Father; His God can be our God.

Thus, the Holy Spirit's work ultimately revolves around the person and work of Jesus Christ. Apart from Him there can be no reconciliation; apart from Him we cannot be restored into a Father-child relationship with God. Jesus underscores this when He says, "He shall glorify me: for he shall receive of mine, and shall shew it unto you" (John 16:14).

The Lord Jesus Christ will ever be the great focal point of the comforting ministry of the Holy Spirit. Isaiah prophesied this regarding the Lord Jesus Christ, and Jesus, in Luke 4, opens the Scriptures to Isaiah 61, saying, "The Spirit of the Lord is upon me...to heal the brokenhearted." Here we have the affirmation of what Christ says in the second beatitude: "To comfort all that mourn; to appoint unto them that mourn in Zion, to give unto them beauty for ashes, the oil of joy for mourning, the garment of praise for the spirit of heaviness" (Isa. 61:2–3). Isaiah prophesied that this would be the essence of the Messiah's ministry, which He would achieve through the Holy Spirit, the Comforter.

Consequently, all of God's servants are given this great commission: "Comfort ye, comfort ye my people, saith your God. Speak ye comfortably to Jerusalem…for she hath received from the LORD's hand double for all her sins" (Isa. 40:1–2). Preachers, as God's spokesmen, have to be faithful in proclaiming the gospel to you over and over again. They must therefore declare to every believer that in Jesus Christ they have received double for all of their sins. Since we have a double problem as sinners (being guilty and filthy), God has provided a double remedy in Christ. In 1 John 2:1–2 we read, "If any man sin, we have an advocate with the Father, Jesus Christ, the righteous: and he is the propitiation for our sins." Already in the Old Testament, God had appointed the morning and evening sacrifice. He knew that His people would sin daily, and He wanted them to understand that there was a daily and double remedy for sin.

Thus, when we succumb to sin, we should not remain there but rather flee to the Lord Jesus Christ, our Advocate with the Father in heaven. When our indwelling corruption troubles us, that wretched and polluting fountain within, the Spirit will comfort us by directing us to Christ, in whom a fountain has been opened against sin and all uncleanness (Zech. 13:1). When we grieve over our lack of conformity to Christ, the Holy Spirit will comfort us by reminding us that we are accepted in the Beloved (Eph. 1:6). When we grieve over our unbelief, the Spirit will comfort us by reminding us of the wonderful truth that even our unbelief cannot annul the faithfulness of God. "If we believe not, yet he abideth faithful: he cannot deny himself" (2 Tim. 2:13).

The Holy Spirit will ever comfort us, as recorded in Isaiah 51:3: "For the LORD shall comfort Zion...; joy and gladness shall be found therein." That explains what Paul means in 2 Corinthians 6:10: "As sorrowful, yet alway rejoicing; ...as having nothing, and yet possessing all things." There you hear the confession of a man who mourns and knows himself to be poor in spirit—sorrowful and mourning, yet always rejoicing because of the comforting work of the Holy Spirit. Thus, Isaiah could prophesy, "And the ransomed of the LORD shall return, and come to Zion with songs and everlasting joy upon their heads: they shall obtain joy and gladness, and sorrow and sighing shall flee away" (Isa. 35:10).

Dear believer, the day is coming that you will mourn and weep no more. God will then wipe away all tears from your eyes, and there shall be no more death, neither sorrow nor crying. Believer, you have a sinless future before you. The day of your complete deliverance is coming, when you shall mourn no more. Blessed indeed are they that mourn, because they shall be forever comforted!

Reader, if you know nothing of that mourning, that grieving over your sin and indwelling corruption, these words of Jesus are then applicable to you: "Woe unto you that laugh now! for ye shall mourn and weep" (Luke 6:25). That's what hell will be—a place where men and women will be weeping and gnashing with their teeth. There you will weep forever and never be comforted—never! How wretched are those who laugh now and who shall weep forever!

God forbid that this would be applicable to either you or me. Therefore, dear reader, have no rest until you know yourself to be one of God's people as described here in the Beatitudes. James 4:8–9 says, "Cleanse your hands, ye sinners; and purify your hearts, ye double minded. Be afflicted, and mourn, and weep: let your laughter be turned into mourning, and your joy to heaviness." In that way, you will learn that you need the Lord Jesus Christ. In that way, you will be led to the comfort that is to be found in Christ alone. Only in that way will this beatitude become applicable to you: "Blessed are they that mourn: for they shall be comforted."

Discussion Questions

1. What is the significant relationship between the first beatitude (being poor in spirit) and the second beatitude (mourning)?

2. What is the importance of the fact that the type of mourning Christ is referring to here is comparable to the kind of mourning one observes at the funeral of a loved one?

3. Why is it that the true Christian will be mourning all the days of his life?

4. Why must we make a distinction between the mourning of which Christ is speaking here and the shedding of physical tears? What can happen if we fail to make that distinction?

5. Why is this spiritual mourning an essential component of that disposition of heart that causes one to hunger and thirst after the righteousness of the Lord Jesus Christ?

6. What is meant by the statement that the Spirit of God both wounds and heals?

7. Why is 2 Corinthians 6:10 such an accurate description of the true Christian: "As sorrowful, yet alway rejoicing; …as having nothing, and yet possessing all things"?

Chapter 3

THE MEEK PRONOUNCED BLESSED

Blessed are the meek;
for they shall inherit the earth.
—MATTHEW 5:5

The longer one studies great paintings, the more fascinating details one will discover. Art lovers can stand for hours before a famous painting and become engrossed with all its nuances. Such is also the case with the spiritual portrait the Lord Jesus Christ has painted for us in the Beatitudes—a precise and profound sevenfold portrait of the Christian. Thus far we have examined two of the main features of that portrait: the blessedness of the poor in spirit and of them that mourn.

We observed that Jesus begins by defining the inner disposition of true Christians: they will always be conscious of their spiritual poverty and will always grieve over their sinfulness. We will now proceed to consider the third trait of this verbal portrait—namely, that as mourning sinners, Christians will also be meek. This will complete Christ's description of the inner disposition that culminates in a hungering and thirsting after righteousness (addressed in the fourth and central beatitude).

As we focus on this third trait of meekness, we will first address the gracious character of the meek, which is not found in the natural man but rather is a trait of regenerating grace. Second, we will discuss the blessed inheritance of the meek, for Christ tells us that they shall inherit the earth.

The Gracious Character of the Meek

No one will ever manifest the meekness that Jesus speaks of here unless he is experientially acquainted with his spiritual poverty. This meekness is therefore utterly foreign to the natural man. In conversation, the word *meek* is commonly used to describe someone whom we consider to be a pushover. One will often say, "Such and such a person is as meek as a lamb." We usually don't mean this in a flattering way.

However, Christ is not speaking of such meekness or weakness. Rather, Christ says that a believer's meekness will be a tangible fruit of the Holy Spirit's ministry within the soul. In Galatians 5:23, Paul defines meekness as being one of the Spirit's fruits, for we are by nature anything but meek. Fallen man is preoccupied with himself. He loves himself, worships himself, seeks himself, and cares only about himself. Men are by nature proud, arrogant, boastful, and narcissistic. Their disposition will be the opposite of what Christ describes here, for by nature we are blind to God's greatness, holiness, and majesty.

In this beatitude, however, Christ says that His people, rather than thinking highly of themselves, think highly of God. This is a preeminent feature of the meekness Christ is defining for us. This mind-set will be the fruit of becoming aware of who God is. When God becomes real in our lives, we will stand in awe of God rather than ourselves!

When we begin to see ourselves as God sees us, all pride, arrogance, and boastfulness will vanish. We will then take our proper place before Him. Such a mind-set was utterly absent in the heart of the Pharisee in the parable of the publican and Pharisee. Although he thought of himself as the quintessence of godliness, he was utterly blind to who he really was before God. Not one shred of meekness could be found in this man; he was thoroughly impressed with himself. Instead of humbling himself, he told God that He should be thankful for a man like him—a man not like others.

The publican, however, had learned to see himself as God saw him. He did not even dare to lift up his eyes; rather, he smote his breast and humbly cried out, "God be merciful to me a sinner." One of the evidences of the grace of God is genuine humility, which flows from meekness. Consequently, when we begin to see ourselves as God sees us, we will come down from our pedestals and take our proper place in the dust before Him.

We clearly see such a manifestation of God's grace in the life of David. Although he had fallen deeply into sin, rather than killing Nathan when he came and boldly said, "Thou art the man"—as any king would have done to someone who had dared to accuse him—David humbled himself. At that moment, he saw his sin in light of who God is, and that caused the great king of Israel to humble himself deeply before God.

Thus, the meekness of the Christian is an appropriate and biblically informed fear of God. The Bible frequently speaks of this fear. He who fears God will show awe, respect, submission, and humility before God. A meek person does not stand in awe of men or himself; rather, he stands in awe of God.

Several scriptural examples will illustrate such meekness. Abraham was a great and mighty man, yet when he was in the presence of God, prayerfully wrestling for Lot and his family and the preservation of Sodom, he addressed God with meekness, saying, "I have taken upon me to speak unto the LORD, which am but dust and ashes" (Gen. 18:27). There is not a whiff of either any pride or arrogance, and all he could say is, "Lord, I am but dust and ashes."

Moses was not naturally easygoing and mild. He had a fiery temperament. Think of how he responded when he saw an Egyptian abusing one of his fellow Israelites. He killed that Egyptian! Later, in the wilderness, Moses became angry with the rebellion of his own people. In a moment of anger, rather than speaking to the rock as God had commanded, he took a rod and smote the rock. His natural inclination in unguarded moments was still to explode in anger.

Yet what does Scripture say about Moses? "Now the man Moses was very meek, above all the men which were upon the face of the earth" (Num. 12:3). How did a man with this fiery nature become the meekest man on earth? The answer is that Moses became acquainted with God! He had spent forty years alone in the wilderness, and there God cured him of all pride and arrogance. Then, at the end of that period, God appeared to him in a burning bush on Mount Horeb, where he was told to take off his shoes, for he was standing on holy ground.

Later, after he had led Israel out of Egypt, Moses met God again when twice he ascended Mount Sinai (Horeb). That experience was so extraordinary that when Moses descended from the mountain, he had to cover his face because of the emanating glory of God. He had seen the glory of God, and those unforgettable experiences transformed Moses into a meek and humble man. He had seen himself against the background of God's glory and majesty!

Scripture tells us that God described Job as a man of remarkable godliness. Yet Job, too, had to learn in a very painful way that he was a sinful man. When God permitted Satan to take away his riches, his children, and his health, and when his friends mistakenly assumed that God was punishing Job for his wickedness, his unsanctified flesh reared its ugly head. Sadly, near the end of the book, he was still justifying himself. He was angry and did not think he was deserving of all that was happening to him.

But then, toward the very end, everything changed. Why? God summoned Job to appear before Him, saying, "Who is this that darkeneth counsel by words without knowledge? Gird up now thy loins like a man; for I will demand of thee, and answer thou me" (Job 38:2–3). He was unable to answer a single question, and by the time God was finished speaking, all Job could say was, "Behold, I am vile; what shall I answer thee?" (Job 40:4). As a result of that encounter with God, Job saw himself as God saw him, compelling him to take his proper place before God. In Job 42:6, he no longer speaks highly of himself, justifies himself, or defends himself. A meek Job now confesses, "I abhor myself, and repent in dust and ashes." When God's Spirit works savingly in our lives, Job's confession will also become an experiential reality for us. God will teach us that essential lesson to make room in our hearts for the gospel and for His only begotten Son, the Lord Jesus Christ.

Isaiah, called to be a prophet, had a remarkable vision in the temple of God's majesty and glory (Isa. 6). The manifestation of God's glory was such that the pillars of the temple were trembling. When Isaiah saw this extraordinary display, he said, "Woe is me! for I am undone...for mine eyes have seen the King, the LORD of hosts." That vision transformed Isaiah into a meek and humble man!

How about Peter, who could be so bold and arrogant—who had even briefly walked on water? In Luke 5, Christ commanded him to cast forth his net again after he and his fellow disciples had not caught anything after fishing all night. After Peter reluctantly obeyed this command, the net was so full that it would certainly have broken if he had not gotten some help. At that moment, Peter saw a glimpse of the divine glory of the Lord Jesus Christ, and he said in astonishment, "Depart from me; for I am a sinful man, O Lord" (Luke 5:8). That will be our response when God becomes real to us. A bold and impetuous Peter became a meek man!

What about Saul of Tarsus, the proud, boastful, brilliant, and arrogant Pharisee? These religious leaders thought very highly of themselves, and so did Saul, who once viewed himself as a Pharisee of the Pharisees. In his own mind, he towered above all his peers—until he met the exalted Christ on the road to Damascus. He then fell to the ground and cried out, "Lord, what wilt thou have me to do?" (Acts 9:6). Saul of Tarsus became a meek man. A genuine and experiential encounter with God will transform proud sinners.

When God, by His Spirit, works savingly in our hearts, He will cause us to become acquainted with Himself so that nothing of our pride, arrogance, or boastfulness will remain. When He compels us to take our proper place, we will realize that as guilty and bankrupt sinners we cannot stand before Him. In Psalm 130:3 the psalmist says, "If thou, LORD, shouldest mark iniquities, O Lord, who shall stand?" David here confessed that if God were to hold him accountable for his life, his actions, and his sins, he could not stand before Him for one moment. God will lead all of His children to the point that this will also become their confession— whatever the unique circumstances of their lives may be.

Keep in mind that Christ here delineates what all Christians have in common. Whether I am a Timothy that fears God from his youth or a Saul of Tarsus, whether I am a David or a Manasseh, whether I am a John or a Levi, or whether I am a Lydia or a jailor, all believers will be taught by the Holy Spirit to humble themselves before God and confess, "Enter not into judgment with thy servant: for in thy sight shall no man living be justified" (Ps. 143:2). Unless there is such an experiential awareness of who God is, and that He "will by no means clear the guilty" (Ex. 34:7), we will never see our need for the Savior and hunger and thirst after Him and His righteousness.

But when that need becomes an experiential reality, Christ will become so precious to our souls. We will then behold His beauty as the all-sufficient, suitable, willing, and able Savior of sinners. As a meek and humble sinner, I will see in Him exactly what I need. I will then hunger and thirst after Jesus as a most precious Redeemer, so that in Him I may be restored into a right relationship with God.

As the Holy Spirit increasingly sheds light on who we are in ourselves, Jesus will become more precious and we will hunger and thirst after His righteousness. We will increasingly learn to trust in nothing other than Jesus Christ and Him crucified. Therefore, the beatitude of meekness will never be present without the traits of the other beatitudes. Only those who are poor in spirit, who mourn, and who are meek will experience salvation. We therefore read in Psalm 147:6, "The LORD lifteth up the meek," and in Psalm 149:4, "He will beautify the meek with salvation."

Meekness is also an abiding spiritual character trait and thus one of the components of Christlikeness. Christ did not often give a description of Himself. However, He did say one thing about Himself in Matthew 11:29: "Take my yoke upon you, and learn of me; for I am meek and lowly in heart: and ye shall find rest unto your souls." The Lord Jesus Christ perfectly manifested that meekness in his humanity, living in perfect submission to His heavenly Father. He honored His heavenly Father, and as the Mediator He knew His proper place at all times.

And so this meekness, this humble disposition of heart—the humbleness that flows out of living in *coram Deo*, or in the presence of God—means we live our lives in the experiential awareness of God's omnipresence. When we live in that awareness, we will be a meek people. Recognizing how gracious God has been to us will render us gentle, patient, and forgiving toward others. When we learn to take our proper place before God, we will also be content with the circumstances of life that God has sovereignly decreed for us.

We need to understand, however, that biblical and gracious meekness does not make us pushovers. Instead, our reverential awe for God and His Word will motivate us to take a strong stand for Him. To be truly meek means that when our own name and reputation are at stake, we will behave as lambs, whereas when God's name and reputation are at stake, we will behave as lions. By nature, the reverse will be true. When someone offends us, we will respond like lions, and when God's name is taken in vain, we behave like lambs. However, when God becomes real and we live in *coram Deo*, our names will no longer matter. Then only God's name and honor will matter.

Therefore, when Moses came down from the mountain, he cast the tablets of the law on the ground—not because he was being either dishonored or offended but because he witnessed how greatly the people were dishonoring God. Having just been in the presence of God, he was meek and therefore filled with holy anger. When Jesus saw merchants turning the house of God into a carnal place of business, He overturned their tables. Why? Because He, as the personification of meekness, was preoccupied with the honor of His Father, saying, "Ye have made it a den of thieves" (Matt. 21:13). Thus, meekness does not mean weakness!

The Blessed Inheritance of the Meek

Jesus attaches a wonderful promise to His beatitude about meekness: "They shall inherit the earth." What a remarkable and fitting promise indeed, for the experientially meek person will honor God, the Creator of heaven of earth, and render Him His worthy praise. Thus, Christ says that the meek—those who acknowledge God for who He is—shall inherit the earth.

Such was the inheritance God gave our first parents! When He created Adam and Eve in the state of rectitude, He gave them the earth as their inheritance. He commanded them to work and beautify the earth that had been especially created for their habitation and benefit. When they fell, however, that earth was subjected to God's curse. It began to produce thorns and thistles, for God said, "Thorns also and thistles shall it bring forth to thee; and thou shalt eat the herb of the field; in the sweat of thy face shalt thou eat bread, till thou return unto the ground; for out of it wast thou taken: for dust thou art, and unto dust shalt thou return" (Gen. 3:18–19).

But Jesus says that the meek citizens of His spiritual kingdom shall again inherit the earth. They are a content people, even when they do not possess the riches this world has to offer. They understand in some measure that their time here below is but a brief preparation for their eternal residence in the new heaven and earth. The grace of God will therefore begin to cure the meek from lusting after the riches of this life. It will redirect their entire focus, teaching them that their real riches are to be found in Christ—and thus in God Himself.

Christ says that the meek have a blessed and extraordinary future, for the day will dawn when there will be a new heaven and a new earth in which righteousness will dwell, and God's redeemed people will be its inhabitants. By a mighty act of His creative power, God will completely refurbish the entire universe and restore this earth, which is now groaning under the curse of sin. Christ is pointing to the great goal of redemption, saying that the people of His kingdom will experience complete restoration.

Man, after all, was the crown jewel of God's creative work. No creature in the entire universe so beautifully displayed God's glory as man, who was created in the image of His only begotten Son. Christ is thus affirming that His people shall forever be the crown jewels of God's redeeming work. They will inherit the new earth in which righteousness will dwell.

The citizens of God's kingdom are therefore called to be strangers and pilgrims in this world. The more Christlike or meek we become, the less this life and this world will mean to us. We will realize that our ultimate destination is this new earth. That is why God will wean us from this present life, so that ultimately we will desire to depart and be with Christ, which is far better. To achieve this, God sometimes has to use the scourge of affliction, especially for all who live in such a remarkably prosperous and comfortable culture as ours. God will therefore cause the meek to long for the inheritance that awaits the people of God.

Remarkably, the Greek word translated as "inherit" refers to the receiving of one's inheritance by lot. When the children of Israel arrived into Canaan (the physical Canaan being a picture of the heavenly Canaan), they received a specific portion of that land by lot: "By lot was their inheritance" (Josh. 14:2). In biblical times, the casting of lots was considered very important. Those who believed in God trusted the casting of the lot, knowing that God Himself would direct it. When Joshua could not understand why Israel had been defeated by Ai, God directed him to cast the lot to determine who it was that had sinned (Joshua 7). The casting of the lot was directed by God Himself, for "the lot is cast into the lap; but the whole disposing thereof is of the LORD" (Prov. 16:33).

Therefore, when the Israelites had finally settled in their new home, the land of Canaan, every Israelite knew a particular section of land to be theirs because God had directed it so. The godly Naboth, for example, would not sell his property to King Ahab, for he knew that his property was his by divine direction.

By using the word *inherit*, Christ thus infers that the blessing to be bestowed on the meek has its origin in God's eternal and sovereign good pleasure. The meek shall inherit the earth because the lot has eternally fallen on them. What a remarkable affirmation that there is no reason to be found in the meek that they should receive such an inheritance! Nothing in ourselves makes us worthy of such an inheritance. If there is anyone who understands that, it will be the graciously meek person! The meeker we are, the more we will see ourselves as God sees us, and so much the more we will understand that nothing in ourselves renders us worthy of such a salvation and redemption, culminating in inheriting the earth.

Believer, when the day dawns that you will eternally inherit the earth, you will receive your inheritance by lot.

Paul therefore writes in Ephesians 1:11–12, "In whom also we have obtained an inheritance, being predestinated according to the purpose of him who worketh all things after the counsel of his own will: that we should be to the praise of his glory, who first trusted in Christ." There you have it! They who are poor in spirit, mourn over their sins, and are meek will receive an inheritance because they have eternally been predestined to receive it. The apostle Peter speaks of an inheritance "reserved in heaven for you" (1 Peter 1:4).

Who stands in awe of this? The graciously meek! They understand experientially that there is no reason in them whatsoever why they should inherit the earth. They will increasingly understand that there is but one explanation: their citizenship is rooted solely in the sovereign good pleasure of a triune God. Christ highlights this when He speaks of the final judgment: "Come, ye blessed of my Father, inherit the kingdom prepared for you from the foundation of the world" (Matt. 25:34). The meek shall inherit the kingdom; they shall inherit the earth.

Dear reader, will you belong to that number? Do you already belong to the people of God? Do you recognize yourself in this verbal portrait the Lord Jesus Christ is giving us? Are the distinctive marks of citizenship in God's kingdom also descriptive of your internal disposition? Do you understand experientially what it means to hunger and thirst after Christ and His righteousness because you are poor in spirit, mournful, and meek? Is this what makes Christ so precious to your soul?

Unless you are a believer by these biblical standards, you will not inherit the earth. Paul said, "Flesh and blood cannot inherit the kingdom of God" (1 Cor. 15:50). If we live and die as we are born, we will not inherit the earth. As stated earlier, each beatitude implies a curse. Thus, cursed are they who are not poor in spirit, who do not mourn, who are not meek, and who do not hunger and thirst after righteousness. If you die as you are born, as an unbeliever, you will inherit hell. You will hear out of the same mouth of Christ, "Depart from me, ye cursed, into everlasting fire, prepared for the devil and his angels" (Matt 25:41). That is the inescapable future for all who do not fear God.

Be not deceived by what the world admires, because what the world esteems highly is despised by God. Our culture says that blessed are they who inherit this earth. However, God says that the meek are blessed, for they, and they alone, shall inherit the kingdom of heaven.

This meekness should be one of the ornaments of the believer's life. We read in Colossians 3:12, "Put on therefore, as the elect of God, holy and beloved…meekness," and in Ephesians 4:1–2 Paul says, "Walk worthy of the vocation wherewith ye are called, with all lowliness and meekness." Such meekness will manifest itself only when we abide in Christ. The more we abide in Him, the meeker we will become, and the more we will begin to resemble the Lord Jesus Christ.

Blessed indeed are the meek, for as inheritors of the earth they will be able to say with profound gratitude for God's sovereign and distinguishing grace, Thou "hast made us unto our God kings and priests: and we shall reign on the earth" (Rev. 5:10).

Discussion Questions

1. What is the connection between the meekness of which Jesus speaks and the fear of God?

2. How does the meekness of the believer differ from the meekness of an unregenerate man who appears to have such a disposition?

3. Why is the meekness of this beatitude such an essential component of the inner disposition that causes a sinner to hunger and thirst after the righteousness of the Lord Jesus Christ?

4. Why will this biblical meekness always yield genuine humility?

5. How do we know that this meekness is also an essential component of the Christlikeness of the true believer?

6. How does the phrase "and they shall inherit the earth" point us to the total restoration aspect of Christ's redeeming work?

7. What is the connection between "and they shall inherit the earth" and the doctrine of predestination?

8. Why will only the meek truly marvel at the doctrine of predestination?

Chapter 4

A BLESSED YEARNING FOR RIGHTEOUSNESS

*Blessed are they which do hunger and thirst
after righteousness: for they shall be filled.*
—MATTHEW 5:6

Having considered the inner and abiding disposition of the Christian, we will now examine the core trait of the citizens of God's kingdom: hungering and thirsting after righteousness.

Here Christ addresses the ongoing and repeated spiritual exercise of the true believer who knows himself to be poor in spirit, mourns over this poverty, and is meek. Such experiential awareness will issue forth in a blessed yearning for righteousness. As we examine this core trait of the Christian, we will consider the object of this yearning, its nature, and its outcome.

The Object of Yearning: Righteousness

This fourth beatitude is the linchpin in the initial seven beatitudes. To use an analogy, it is the axle around which the entire wheel of Christian experience revolves. All the other beatitudes are connected to this central beatitude. The inward disposition delineated in the first three beatitudes will cause us to hunger and thirst after righteousness, and when we are filled to overflowing with righteousness, it will spill over into our lives and cause us to be merciful, pure in heart, and peacemakers.

As has already been stated, the order in which Christ pronounces the Beatitudes is not arbitrary. Each beatitude presumes the previous one and anticipates the next. Thus, the hungering and thirsting that Jesus refers to is not randomly inserted. Those who hunger and thirst after righteousness know why they are yearning for it. The Spirit of God so works in the hearts of Christians that such yearning becomes their only option. They who are poor in spirit, who mourn, and who are meek have learned intellectually and experientially that they need exactly the righteousness that Christ is speaking of.

What is Christ referring to when He speaks of righteousness? The word *righteousness* readily yields its own meaning. In English, righteousness simply means *that which is right*. Thus, Christ is saying, "Blessed are they who yearn after that which is right."

By what standard do we determine what is right or not? What is righteousness or unrighteousness? The Bible gives us only one standard: God's holy law. The moral law defines for us what is right in God's sight. Whatever contradicts that law is unrighteous. Since God is a righteous God, He has given us a righteous standard.

Adam, and initially Eve, lived in perfect harmony with the law of God written on their hearts. In other words, everything about them was right. They had a right relationship with God that completely conformed to His will for them. As a result of that right relationship, they also lived a right life—one in perfect conformity to their Creator's revealed will. Their chief desire was to live righteously, thereby pleasing their Maker.

Since Adam and Eve had a right relationship with God and lived a right life, they were righteous in the double sense of the word. Everything about them was right, and because they were holy and sinless, they were completely compatible with a holy and righteous God. In our computer-driven society, the word *compatibility* is used frequently. We all understand that a computer and its peripheral devices must be compatible for them to function properly. Thus, if your printer is incompatible with your computer, your printer will not work. By way of analogy, we can say that when God created us in Adam, we were fully compatible with Him. But as a result of our deep fall, everything about us has become unrighteous. Consequently, we no longer have a proper or righteous relationship with our Creator. By nature, we live apart from God, for in Adam we divorced ourselves from Him.

As a result of that broken relationship, we no longer live righteously. Every aspect of our lives now contradicts the perfect standard of God's law. As fallen creatures, we are now incompatible with God. Adam and Eve, and all their posterity, were expelled from the sacred territory of the Garden of

Eden because a holy and righteous God cannot tolerate an unrighteous creature in His presence.

The amazing truth of the gospel, however, is that God has provided unrighteous sinners with a righteousness by which we can again become acceptable in His sight. By nature we are just as blind as the Pharisee who stood in the front of the temple praising himself, thoroughly impressed with his own righteousness and totally ignorant of how abominable he was in God's sight. We need to understand that God can be satisfied only with perfection. In other words, God's requirement of us has not changed. He requires perfect, flawless righteousness. Anything less than that is unacceptable. That is why Jesus said, "Except your righteousness shall exceed the righteousness of the scribes and Pharisees, ye shall in no case enter into the kingdom of heaven" (Matt. 5:20). Unless we are perfectly and flawlessly righteous, God can neither accept us, receive us, nor embrace us.

The Holy Spirit's ministry is to confront us with our lack of such flawless righteousness. In essence, Christ is saying, "All spiritual life begins with the awareness of one's spiritual poverty, for blessed are the poor in spirit." We will never desire the righteousness that God provides in His only begotten Son unless we are thoroughly convinced in our hearts that we completely lack that righteousness. We must understand what Isaiah meant when he said, "But we are all as an unclean thing, and all our righteousnesses are as filthy rags" (Isa. 64:6).

That's a strong statement. Isaiah is saying that God views our righteousness as filthy rags—as a menstrual cloth. Hence, our very best works are unacceptable to God. The poor publican in the parable—who dared not come to the front of the temple, who dared not lift up his eyes, and who smote on his breast—was aware of his bankruptcy before God. Such experiential awareness of one's spiritual poverty is the work of the Holy Spirit, for we will never be inclined naturally to acknowledge this. We may casually agree with the fact that we are sinners, but we will never acknowledge that we have absolutely nothing that measures up to God's standard of perfect righteousness.

It should be noted again that all the spiritual attributes articulated in the Beatitudes are never found in the natural man. They will never be components of one's natural disposition. These seven marks will manifest themselves only as a result of the marvelous work of the Holy Spirit. Only His irresistible and transforming ministry will cause a sinner to acknowledge that he is bankrupt, that all he has is unrighteousness. That experiential awareness will cause the citizens of God's kingdom to hunger and thirst after the righteousness He has provided in His only begotten Son.

Why do Christians yearn for that righteousness? This desire proceeds from God shedding abroad His love into our hearts. From that moment on, our hearts will yearn after God. How we will then grieve over the fact that our sin separates us from God! That sorrowful awareness will cause us to yearn for a righteousness that will bring us back into a right relationship with God—a righteousness that will so restore us that we again begin to live a right life unto God. That is the righteousness God unveils for us in His Word and in the gospel, setting before us and offering to us the righteousness of His only begotten Son, the Lord Jesus Christ.

During His sojourn on earth, Jesus merited a perfect righteousness by living a life of flawless obedience to the law of God. His perfect obedience was completely acceptable to His Father. However, He also accomplished something else. By His death on the cross, He paid the full penalty for our breaking of the law, thereby fully satisfying the claims of God's offended justice and paving the way for full reconciliation with Him. He merited that righteousness by living a life we, as sinners, never could have lived, and by dying a death that we never could have died. J. C. Ryle, a well-known British preacher, said, "Christ has saved us by His doing and by His dying." By His doing and His dying—by His active and passive obedience—Christ has merited a perfect and flawless righteousness that is fully acceptable to His Father. Thus, when He cried out, "It is finished," His Father immediately rent the veil, thereby demonstrating that He is completely pleased with the finished work of His beloved Son.

In the gospel, God freely and unconditionally offers to us His Son and His flawless righteousness—the righteousness God demands and we cannot produce. He promises that upon believing in His only begotten Son He will impute to us that flawless righteousness. That simply means that He will credit Christ's righteousness to our bankrupt account. On the basis of that imputed righteousness, a just God will declare the believing sinner righteous—not because he has any righteousness of his own but rather because God has graciously bestowed on him the righteousness He demands!

Dear reader, have you learned to understand that you need that divinely provided righteousness and that you need precisely such a savior, the Lord Jesus Christ? By nature we have no need of such a Christ. The gospel offends the natural man, for it plainly declares that before God we are spiritually bankrupt and void of all righteousness.

However, against that background, the gospel also reveals that Jesus Christ provides the perfect righteousness needed to have a right relationship with God. The Lord Jesus Christ will therefore become so precious to sinners. When we have been emptied of all that is of ourselves, when we are confronted with the ugly reality of our sin, and when the Spirit confronts us with the reality that we cannot make things right with God, how exceedingly precious the Lord Jesus Christ will then become! The Lord therefore describes the citizens of His kingdom as those who hunger and thirst after *that* righteousness.

The Nature of the Yearning: Hungering and Thirsting

We will now discuss the nature of this yearning. Christ again uses carefully chosen words to describe this desire as hungering and thirsting. Everyone understands these words. We have all been so hungry that we could hardly wait to eat, and we have all been so thirsty—especially on a hot summer day—that we could hardly wait to get into the house to get something to drink.

We all recognize hunger and thirst as basic human desires that must be satisfied. We cannot permanently live with hunger. Ultimately, it will become so intense that we will do whatever it takes to find something to satisfy it. In the Netherlands, during the "hunger winter" of 1944 and 1945, people were so hungry that they would eat flower bulbs and go to soup kitchens to secure a very watered-down version of soup. Children would be waiting for empty soup barrels to be thrown out the door, and they would then literally dive into those barrels to lick its walls clean. That's how hungry they were! Hunger is a desire that must be satisfied.

The same is true for thirst. When our throat becomes parched, we will do anything to quench that thirst. We cannot live without these basic desires being satisfied. God obviously created our bodies in such a way that we will desire that which we need to live. In other words, hungering and thirsting belong to the most essential and fundamental desires of our existence. Every single day we will take the necessary steps to satisfy our hunger and thirst.

Christ uses this analogy to illustrate the spiritual yearning expressed in this beatitude. Jesus declares that the people of God's kingdom will yearn after Him and His righteousness; their desire will be such that they cannot be satisfied unless that yearning is satisfied. In other words, true believers cannot be satisfied with anything other than the righteousness that they yearn for so intensely. They cannot be satisfied unless they acquire a righteousness that brings them into a right and reconciled relationship with God and equips them to begin living a life that is pleasing to Him.

As is true in the natural realm, one cannot just pretend to be spiritually hungry and thirsty. Those desires are real. One can tell whether people are genuinely hungry and thirsty.

Thus, Christ teaches here that this yearning after righteousness is not merely an intellectual exercise. Rather, He is saying that this yearning is deeply experiential—something that becomes very real to the citizens of God's kingdom.

That desire ultimately issues forth from a true Christian yearning after the living God Himself. The psalmist therefore said, "As the hart panteth after the water brooks, so panteth my soul after thee, O God" (Ps. 42:1). That yearning for reconciliation with God makes a believer intensely hungry and thirsty for the righteousness found in the Lord Jesus Christ. Such yearning is expressed in the words of the Dutch poet Jacob Groenewegen: "Give me Jesus, or else I die." Nothing can satisfy a living soul except Jesus Christ and His righteousness.

Reader, do you recognize yourself in this? The circumstances of your conversion may be as diverse as those of Lydia and the jailor, or of Timothy and Paul. However, all believers will have this in common: a deep yearning for Christ Himself. Jesus expressed this clearly in John 6:45: "Every man therefore that hath heard, and hath learned of the Father, cometh unto me." Jesus says that we can know whether we have been taught by His Father when we, by faith, come to Him. Sinners taught by the Father will be irresistibly drawn to Christ and His righteousness.

The Holy Spirit will achieve this by stripping us of our self-made righteousness. He will so confront us with our spiritual poverty that the Lord Jesus Christ will become irresistible to our soul. The Spirit will make Jesus irresistibly attractive so that we cannot stay away from Him; our whole being will yearn after Him and His flawless righteousness. The believer will understand experientially that only in Christ can he be reconciled to God and restored into His favor. In Him alone can God's image be restored again in his life. Only in Him will he be equipped to begin living a life that is pleasing to God.

We need to recognize that the true believer also yearns for the latter. He will desire not only to have a right relationship with God but also to live a life that is pleasing to Him—a righteous life. Using theological terms, Christ is saying that they are blessed who do hunger and thirst after Him for their justification and sanctification—for imputed and imparted righteousness. Both foundational benefits of redemption are wrapped up in the word *righteousness* as it used here by Christ. These benefits are inseparable; one will never occur without the other. True Christians yearn for both.

This is expressed in Romans 7. Here the apostle Paul expressed his spiritual grief, for in the innermost recesses of his being he wished to obey God's law—not to earn God's favor but rather as an expression of love. Yet it grieved him that he found himself coming short of what the law requires. Therefore he groaned within himself and made the painful confession that in his flesh dwelt no good thing. However, he simultaneously confessed that the delight of his inner man was to obey God's revealed will.

It is an essential mark of spiritual life that the true Christian longs not only to be in Christ and reconciled to God but also to be like Christ. Simply stated, those who come to Christ will also desire to become like Him. Coming to and becoming like Christ belong inseparably together. It is the Christian's abiding desire to become like Christ, having been predestined to be conformed to the image of God's Son (Rom. 8:29).

Dear reader, if such hungering and thirsting is foreign to you, you are lacking the most fundamental mark of true spiritual life. Can you lay your heart bare before God and say, "Lord, Thou knowest all things, Thou knowest that in the deepest recesses of my soul, my heart cries out after Thee; Thou knowest that I desire to be righteous in Thy sight; Thou knowest how much I need Thy Son and His righteousness; Thou knowest how precious Thy Son has become to me"? A true believer ultimately cannot be satisfied with anything but Christ Himself. For the true believer, Christ becomes, and increasingly will be, his all and in all. That is the full satisfaction Christ promises in this beatitude to such hungry and thirsty souls.

The Outcome of This Spiritual Yearning: Full Satisfaction

"And they shall be filled." The grammatical construction implies that the experience of being filled proceeds from a source outside of ourselves. This is not a self-manufactured satisfaction. The Spirit of God who makes and keeps believers hungry and thirsty for Christ and His righteousness will also fill them.

Again, the choice of vocabulary speaks volumes: "They shall be filled." The literal rendering would be that they shall be filled to overflowing. The analogy would be to take a glass and let the water run till it gushes over. That is the sort of filling that Christ promises to the hungering and thirsting citizens of His kingdom—namely, that they shall be filled to overflowing.

This is consistent with what Christ says elsewhere: "I am come that they might have life, and that they might have it more abundantly" (John 10:10). This agrees with the language of Psalm 132:15: "I will abundantly bless her provision: I will satisfy her poor with bread." The very nature of God is to bless His people to overflowing, for, as the Belgic Confession so beautifully states in article 1, He is an overflowing Fountain of good. Thus, any notion that God gives His people only the bare minimum, giving them a crumb now and then, entirely contradicts the Word of God as well as His very nature.

Parents who greatly love their children want to bless them. They want to help their children to the utmost of their ability and will do everything in their power to meet their children's needs. This is infinitely more true in the spiritual realm. The same God who will strip us of all our own righteousness and self-confidence desires to lead us to His only begotten Son, the Lord Jesus Christ, so that we might embrace Him by faith. Embracing His Son by faith so pleases the Father that He will respond by filling the believer to overflowing.

In Psalm 107:9 we read, "For he satisfieth the longing soul, and filleth the hungry soul with goodness," and in Jeremiah 31:14 the Lord says, "And I will satiate the soul of the priests with fatness, and my people shall be satisfied with my goodness." There is nothing that pleases God more than when a sinner finds his joy and satisfaction in His only begotten Son. He is greatly pleased and honored in hearing the echo of His own Word when we say, "O heavenly Father, I too, I am well pleased with Thy only begotten Son."

The true Christian will therefore be unable to find real satisfaction apart from Christ. The Holy Spirit will see to it that we cannot find any peace except in Him. Therefore, if we secretly trust or look for comfort in something other than Christ, He will take it away from us in order to make us rest in Him alone. Christ alone can satisfy the living soul. Once we experience something of that satisfaction, of being filled to overflowing, nothing else will ever be able to satisfy us again.

This hungering and thirsting is a lifelong experience—as are all the Beatitudes. There is again an obvious analogy in the natural realm. Just because we may have had a phenomenal meal one day does not mean that we will not eat the next day. This is consistent with how God made us. Although we find perfect satisfaction in a meal one day, we will hunger and thirst again the next day. Likewise, the life of a believer consists of an ongoing hungering and thirsting after Christ, an ongoing fleeing to Him, an ongoing coming to Him, and an ongoing and repeated experience of those spiritual desires being satisfied only in the person and work of the Lord Jesus Christ. Just as one good meal sets the stage for the next, likewise the more I taste experientially who Christ is, the more I will begin to experience how precious He is, the more I will yearn for Him, and the more I will desire to grow in my knowledge of Him. The apostle Paul, a man who had such an extraordinary knowledge of Christ, yearned for this: "that I may know him, and the power of his resurrection" (Phil. 3:10).

Dear reader, do you recognize yourself in this fundamental mark of the true Christian—this core trait of spiritual life? Does your spiritual life consist chiefly of hungering and thirsting after Christ and His righteousness? If, in all honesty, you would have to conclude that such hungering and thirsting does not yet describe you, I urge you to seek Christ, who, even today, by way of the gospel, offers you the righteousness you need in order to be reconciled to God. Christ is willing and ready to receive the vilest sinner, and He has promised that if you come to Him, you will not be cast out (John 6:37). He tells us in the gospel that even for you there is a perfect robe of righteousness!

Do not be like that man who, after being freely offered the king's robe, entered the wedding feast dressed in his own garment. He placed himself at the table with the guests of the king, who spotted him immediately, and the man was cast out (Matt. 22:11–13).

Dear friend, you cannot appear before God dressed in your own righteousness. God will accept only Christ's righteousness when you and I appear before Him. He freely offers you that robe of righteousness today! He promises you in the gospel that if you believe in His Son and trust in Him, the righteousness He has merited will become yours and will render you acceptable in His sight.

Dear believer, you who hunger and thirst after Christ and His righteousness, the day is coming when the promise of this beatitude will be fulfilled to perfection. You will then be filled to overflowing in a manner that you have never experienced in this life. It will be a day of which we read, "They shall hunger no more, neither thirst any more;... For the Lamb which is in the midst of the throne shall feed them, and shall lead them unto living fountains of waters" (Rev. 7:16–17).

That is the blessed future that awaits all who hunger and thirst after Christ and His righteousness! There will come a day of perfect and everlasting satisfaction. Yet, amazingly, when that day of full consummation arrives, we are told that the Lamb will ever feed His redeemed people and lead them "unto living fountains of waters." He will ever be our complete and everlasting satisfaction, which is why Jesus said, "I am the bread of life: he that cometh to me shall never hunger; and he that believeth on me shall never thirst" (John 6:35).

Discussion Questions

1. What is the connection between the first three beatitudes and "hungering and thirsting after righteousness"?

2. What is Scripture referring to when it uses the word *righteousness*? How does this term relate to Adam prior to his fall—and thus in the state of innocence?

3. What did Jesus mean when He said, "Except your righteousness shall exceed the righteousness of the scribes and Pharisees, ye shall in no case enter into the kingdom of heaven" (Matt. 5:20)?

4. How does the righteousness of this beatitude relate to the person and work of the Lord Jesus Christ?

5. Why do true believers hunger and thirst after the righteousness of the Lord Jesus Christ?

6. What is meant by saying that believers hunger and thirst after *imputed* and *imparted* righteousness?

7. Why did Christ select the words *hunger* and *thirst* to describe the believer's yearning for His righteousness?

8. In what manner will those who hunger and thirst after righteousness be filled?

9. What is the connection between this beatitude and the Lord's Supper?

Chapter 5

THE MERCIFUL
PRONOUNCED BLESSED

Blessed are the merciful:
for they shall obtain mercy.
—MATTHEW 5:7

We have all paged through a picture album and, as we looked at pictures of previous generations, have suddenly been struck by seeing facial traits that remind us of the present generation. Can others observe spiritual traits in us that remind them of the Lord Jesus Christ? If we call ourselves Christians, we are thereby confessing that we wish to be known as people who are Christlike. Is there enough evidence in our lives that others can see the resemblance between the Lord Jesus Christ and us?

Let me illustrate. A godly doctor practiced for years among African natives, doing so prior to the arrival of missionaries. When missionaries began their ministry among them, and one of them began to speak to them about Jesus, describing His gracious character, the native people excitedly exclaimed, "We know Him, we know Him!" The perplexed missionary asked, "How can that be? Christ is no longer here; He is now in heaven at the right hand of the Father." Yet they insisted that they knew Him, exclaiming once more, "We know Him, we know Him!" Curiously he inquired, "How do you know Him? When did you meet Him?" They responded, "As you described Christ for us, we couldn't help but think of a doctor who worked among us and who matches that description exactly." The missionary realized at once that what they had observed in that doctor's life so reminded them of Christ that when He was described to them, they said, "We know Him!"

Could anyone ever say that about us—about my or your life? Our professed Christianity will be of no value unless Christ, in some measure, becomes visible in our lives. Paul tells us in Romans 8:29 that believers have been predestined to be conformed to the image of Christ. This conformity is the preeminent purpose of predestination. Believers have been chosen in Christ to become like Him.

When we are saved by grace, the Holy Spirit unites us to Christ and causes us to embrace Him by faith. As a consequence of that union, we will also begin to look like Christ. As the hallmark of true conversion, such a living union between the Lord Jesus Christ and one's soul cannot but manifest itself. In other words, the same Spirit who dwells in Christ without measure also dwells in the believer. Thus, a real and vital union to Christ will cause us to become like Him. These two foundational truths are inseparably connected. Should such evidence of the transforming and renewing ministry of the Holy Spirit be consistently lacking, our profession of Christ will be refuted by a Christless life.

Jesus therefore ends His Sermon on the Mount with these searching and unsettling words: "Not every one that saith unto me, Lord, Lord, shall enter into the kingdom of heaven; but he that doeth the will of my Father which is in heaven" (Matt. 7:21). In other words, you cannot call Him Lord unless you are also a doer of His Father's will. You cannot claim to belong to Him unless you in some measure also behave like Him.

We see this vital relationship between our union to Christ and our resemblance to Him in the verbal portrait Jesus paints for us in the Beatitudes. Thus far, we have examined what the Christian looks like on the inside—that is, what his inner disposition is like as a fruit of God's gift of a new heart.

Yet this portrait is not complete unless we examine how this inner disposition manifests itself outwardly. With perfect wisdom and profound clarity, Christ brilliantly delineates for us how a new heart will manifest itself in a new life. The function of such a Spirit-wrought inner disposition will manifest itself in godly conduct. He defines such godliness by giving us three fundamental traits of a Christlike life: true believers are merciful or compassionate, they are pure in heart, and they are peacemakers.

We will begin to examine the external affirmation of internal godliness by exploring the fifth beatitude—namely, "Blessed are the merciful: for they shall obtain mercy." First, we will focus on the identity of the merciful. Please note that He is *not* saying, "Blessed are they who do certain things" but rather "Blessed are they who *are* a certain way." Our habitual actions will ultimately prove to be a reflection of our real identity. Second, we will examine the conduct of the merciful, answering the question of how mercy manifests itself in the Christian's walk. Third, we will define the blessedness of the merciful, for, He says, "They shall obtain mercy."

Let me insert here that Christ is by no means teaching that we can merit God's mercy by being merciful; rather, when we display by our lives that we are merciful, we give evidence that we ourselves are the recipients of God's mercy.

The Identity of the Merciful

The direct correlation between how a Christian walks and what lives within his heart becomes evident immediately. Just as Christ clarifies spiritual poverty to be foundational for all spiritual life, and that there will thus be no hungering and thirsting after righteousness unless one recognizes one's poverty, He likewise says that being merciful is also a foundational trait of Christlike conduct. Nothing is a more foundational affirmation of spiritual citizenship than being merciful and compassionate.

When God revealed Himself to Moses in Exodus 34, having promised Moses that He would show him His glory, the first thing He said about Himself was that He is merciful. The Puritan Thomas Watson posits insightfully that mercy is the darling attribute of God—the attribute nearest to His heart. In Exodus 34, God unveiled His glory verbally to Moses, giving him a glimpse into His eternal heart—into that which constitutes the essence of His Being.

How remarkable indeed that the Lord begins His self-revelation by saying that He is merciful and gracious! Since mercy and grace are core attributes of God, it should come as no surprise that Christ here defines being merciful (and gracious) as one of the core attributes of God's children.

Before we unfold how mercy functions in the citizens of God's kingdom, we need to briefly examine the biblical references to the mercy and grace of God in order to understand what Christ means when He describes a Christian as being merciful. We often speak of the divine attributes of mercy and grace interchangeably, for they have much in common. Yet there is a distinct difference. They have in common that when God is merciful and gracious to sinners, He bestows on them His unmerited favor. In other words, God manifests His goodness toward us even though we are undeserving of it. Thus, the words *mercy* and *grace* radically exclude all human merit. How marvelous it is therefore that God reveals Himself to Moses as merciful!

We can understand this only by recognizing that mercy and grace cannot be divorced from the cross of Calvary. Apart from the cross, God could not possibly manifest His goodness to sinners. Since God is infinitely holy, righteous, and perfect, we deserve only His wrath because of our sins. Yet, precisely because God is a God of love, He devised a way in and through His beloved Son whereby He can freely bestow His goodness and unmerited favor on us.

However, as much as mercy and grace have in common the manifestation of God's unmerited favor toward us, there is also a distinction. The focus of God's mercy is goodness toward *wretched* sinners, whereas the focus of grace is on His goodness toward *guilty* sinners. To be a guilty sinner simply means that we deserve to be punished—analogous to a criminal being deserving of punishment upon having been found guilty.

As sinners, we are both wretched and guilty. In Adam's fall we lost everything, for we lost God's image and favor. Consequently, we have become inexpressibly wretched, undone, and poor, and therefore are in need of the mercy of God. Yet since our sins also render us guilty before God, we also need His grace. And God has manifested His goodness to guilty sinners by what Christ has accomplished on the cross!

Furthermore, God's mercy and grace are not merely the manifestation of His unmerited favor toward us; rather, it is also the manifestation of His forfeited favor. In other words, we not only are undeserving of His favor but have also forfeited it, and we do so every single day.

When a sinner takes refuge in Christ, he will, by faith, embrace God's extraordinary provision for his wretched and guilty soul. God promises us in the gospel that when we believe and trust in His beloved Son, the Lord Jesus Christ, He will be merciful and gracious to us. Otherwise stated, He will bestow on us the exact opposite of what we deserve. He did so toward the man who was crucified beside Jesus—a man deserving of hell. Instead, Christ tells him that he is going to be in paradise with Him! As sinners, we deserve God's wrath, yet God declares that if we repent and believe in His Son, He will pardon us and embrace us in His loving arms.

The Conduct of the Merciful

When we experience the reality of God's mercy in Christ toward us, we will be filled to overflowing, something that a true believer will never be able to forget. What believer can forget that moment when he or she, as a blessed consequence of trusting in Christ, experienced in some measure that peace which passes all understanding and that comes from trusting in Christ?

It should be self-evident that when something fills our hearts to overflowing, it will spill over into our lives. Therefore, when believers experience being filled with the wonder of divine and full pardon in Christ, they will have a deep experiential consciousness of the wonder of God's mercy toward them. Consequently, they will have compassion for others, for they will realize that one's fellow man—whether one's spouse, child, colleague, or family member—is equally wretched. When the Spirit of God accomplishes His saving work within us, we will become aware not only that we have a deep spiritual need but also that others are in need of the salvation we have been privileged to experience in Christ. Thomas Watson puts it this way: "True religion begets tenderness. As it melts the heart in contrition towards God, so in bowels of compassion toward others."[1]

Just as natural children will resemble their parents, God's spiritual children will resemble their heavenly Father. Again, I quote Thomas Watson: "God accounts Himself most glorious in the shining robes of mercy. Now by works of mercy

---

1. Thomas Watson, *The Beatitudes* (Edinburgh: Banner of Truth, 1975), 153.

we resemble the God of mercy."[2] Thus, Jesus says that His people's defining feature will be mercy and compassion. You cannot claim to be a Christian unless you are compassionate toward others—that is, unless you feel a burden for the spiritual well-being of others, especially of those close to you. Indeed, if you have experienced the wonder of God's saving mercy toward you in Christ, you will desire that others might be the recipients of that salvation as well. You will then realize what will happen to your loved ones if they should die without having believed on the Lord Jesus Christ. To be merciful is to be burdened with the spiritual and everyday needs of your fellow man.

Thus, mercy is one of the fruits of the Spirit. In Hebrew, the words for mercy and godliness are synonymous. To put it another way, godliness will manifest itself in being merciful, and being merciful will manifest itself in having compassion for the spiritual and physical well-being of one's fellow man. As John asserts, "Whoso hath this world's good, and seeth his brother have need, and shutteth up his bowels of compassion from him, how dwelleth the love of God in him?" (1 John 3:17).

Let's re-read this passage—but now positively: "Whoever hath this world's good, and seeth his brother have need, and openeth up his bowels of compassion toward him, in him dwelleth the love of God." When we behave ourselves as the children of our heavenly Father, we will reveal something of His character. James writes, "But the wisdom that is from above is…full of mercy and good fruits, without par-

---

2. Watson, *Beatitudes*, 162.

tiality, and without hypocrisy" (James 3:17). Paul exhorts, "Put on, therefore, as the elect of God, holy and beloved, bowels of mercy, kindness, humbleness of mind, meekness, longsuffering" (Col. 3:12). Do you recognize the beatitudes in Paul's description?

Being merciful is a fundamental and abiding aspect of Christian living. In addition to having a real concern for the spiritual and temporal welfare of one's neighbor, mercifulness also means that one will be compelled to pray and intercede for one's neighbor. Intercessory prayer is thus an important component of the Christian life. And how could it be any different? When one begins to sense the need of his fellow man, one will be compelled to pray to the God of all mercy that He might be merciful to them as well. Paul therefore writes, "I exhort therefore, that, first of all, supplications, prayers, intercessions, and giving of thanks, be made for all men" (1 Tim. 2:1). In James 5:16 we read, "Pray one for another.... The effectual fervent prayer of a righteous man availeth much."

Christ remarkably demonstrated and exemplified this on the cross. The Savior Himself practiced mercy, for although He was suffering excruciating and unspeakable pain, the spiritual need of His abusers who were nailing Him to the cross was foremost on His mind. His first words uttered on the cross were "Father, forgive them; for they know not what they do" (Luke 23:34). How this affirms that mercy is the darling attribute of God! It was nearest to Jesus' heart! He was making intercession for the transgressors (Isa. 53:12).

The Blessedness of the Merciful

If we wish to claim that we are Christians, we had better be Christlike. Simply put, we too ought to be interceding for others' needs and be ready to forgive our neighbors. Matthew 18 records the parable of the king who had a servant who owed him ten thousand talents of gold. Today the equivalent sum would be about seven to nine billion dollars—a debt that was not payable. Yet, when the servant approached the king, he was forgiven his debt and made a free man. This king was being merciful to his servant, giving him the opposite of what he deserved. The servant who was worthy of being cast into jail for the remainder of his life was instead forgiven.

However, the forgiven servant met a fellow servant who owed him a very small amount. The latter man owed the forgiven servant the equivalent of about twelve thousand dollars. Consider for a moment the vast disparity between the nine billion dollars the servant owed his king versus the twelve thousand dollars this man owed the forgiven servant! Yet the forgiven servant grabbed his fellow servant by the throat and said, "Pay me what you owe me!" When this servant could not pay the forgiven servant, the latter threw him into jail. The fact that his king had been merciful to him seemed to have made no impression at all on this forgiven servant, for he refused to be merciful to others. Jesus concludes the parable by saying that he who is unwilling to forgive those who have trespassed against him will also not be forgiven.

If you are unwilling to be merciful to others, you have never experienced and understood the mercy of God. In the Lord's Prayer, Jesus taught us to ask God to forgive us our trespasses, or debts, as we forgive our debtors—those indebted to us. That is to say, Christ is teaching us that we should not even venture to come to His father, asking Him to forgive our debts, if we are unwilling to forgive the debt of our fellow men.

The same is being implied in this beatitude: if you are unwilling to forgive those who have sinned against you, you have probably never experienced the wonder of divine forgiveness. For when it becomes an experiential reality that God has pardoned you, having canceled your "nine billion dollar" debt when you, by faith, trusted in His Son, how willing you then ought to be to forgive those who have sinned against you!

Being merciful will manifest itself in being ready to forgive others. If God is ready to forgive, then we should also be ready to forgive. As Leviticus 19:18 says, "Thou shalt not avenge, nor bear any grudge against the children of thy people, but thou shalt love thy neighbour as thyself." Are you bearing a grudge toward another person? Are you unwilling to forgive someone who has trespassed against you? If the latter is the case, you had better ask yourself whether you have ever experienced the reality of divine forgiveness, for when you do—when you are overwhelmed with God's mercy toward you—how can you then not be gracious to your fellow man?

That is the point of Jesus' parable! He says that compared to the debt we owe God, the debt our fellow man may owe us is but a mere pittance. Thus, if you are persistently unwilling to forgive those who have sinned against you, you have not experienced the reality of divine forgiveness in your own soul. Paul affirms this in Colossians 3:13: "Forbearing one another, and forgiving one another, if any man have a quarrel against any: even as Christ forgave you, so also do ye."

Being merciful also reveals itself in an attitude of patience toward and unconditional acceptance of one's neighbor. This means that we will be able to endure much. As a merciful person, you will be patient toward others, "with all lowliness and meekness, with longsuffering, forbearing one another in love" (Eph. 4:2). In Proverbs 17:9 we read, "He that covereth a transgression seeketh love."

Christ says that those who display such a disposition are blessed indeed, for they are merciful as their heavenly Father is merciful. Luke 6:36 highlights this: "Be therefore merciful, as your Father also is merciful." Thus, when Jesus says, "they shall obtain mercy," He is saying that the merciful, in the end, will experience God's mercy forever, for the fact that they are merciful proves that they have experienced God's mercy of salvation. Consequently, those who consistently refuse to be merciful show that they have never experienced the mercy of God themselves. Do you recognize yourself as being a merciful person?

If you are not merciful to others, God the Father will also not be merciful to you. "For he shall have judgment without mercy, that hath shewed no mercy" (James 2:13). Christ is not teaching here that believers can lose their salvation. Having said that, however, if you are a believer with unresolved issues between you and your fellow man, you should not be surprised that you are dwelling in spiritual darkness. You will presently not be experiencing the mercy of God, for God will not tolerate His people being unmerciful. Not until we repent and humble ourselves—until, by the grace of God, we again become a merciful people ready to forgive—will we have a fresh experiential sense of God's favor. Micah 6:8 puts it this way: "He hath shewed thee, O man, what is good; and what does the LORD require of thee, but to do justly, and to love mercy, and to walk humbly with thy God?"

Christ underscores this pointedly in the second half of Matthew 25 when He gives us a preview of the final judgment. He tells us that we will be judged by whether we have been merciful. The righteous will say, "Lord, when saw we thee an hungred, and fed thee? or thirsty, and gave thee drink? When saw we thee a stranger, and took thee in? or naked, and clothed thee?" (Matt. 25:37–38). Jesus will then answer, "Inasmuch as ye have done it unto one of the least of these my brethren, ye have done it unto me" (Matt. 25:40).

The ungodly will also ask, "Lord, when saw we thee an hungred, or athirst, or a stranger, or naked, or sick, or in prison, and did not minister unto thee?" (Matt. 25:44). Jesus will remind them that they were never merciful, saying, "Inasmuch as ye did it not to one of the least of these, ye did it not to me" (Matt. 25:45).

That's how important this mark of grace is, and it comes so very close to all of us! Hence, Jesus defines being merciful as the foundational mark of the Christian—how by his life he will show that he truly has a new heart. The disposition of his heart will be revealed through a new life full of mercy toward others. Let us therefore recognize that this is what the Lord requires of us: "to do justly, and to love mercy, and to walk humbly with thy God" (Micah 6:8).

Discussion Questions

1. Since the order of the Beatitudes is not arbitrary, what conclusion can we draw from the fact that Christ posits being merciful as the initial fruit proceeding from being filled with righteousness?

2. How do we know that being merciful is a reflection of God's character?

3. What do mercy and grace have in common, and how do they differ?

4. How do James 3:17 and Colossians 3:12 underscore the importance of this spiritual trait of being merciful?

5. What experiential connection is there between being poor in spirit and being merciful?

6. How does this disposition of being merciful manifest itself in the Christian's conduct toward his neighbor?

7. How did Christ manifest this disposition of being merciful on the cross?

8. Does the fifth beatitude teach that being merciful merits God's mercy? Why or why not?

9. What do Luke 6:36 and Micah 6:8 teach us about being merciful?

Chapter 6

THE PURE IN HEART

Blessed are the pure in heart:
for they shall see God.
—MATTHEW 5:8

So far we have demonstrated how the inner disposition of the Christian, resulting in being filled to overflowing with Christ, will manifest itself outwardly in mercy, purity in heart, and peacemaking. As we have established the connection between being poor in spirit and being merciful, we will now consider how mourning over sin will function in tandem with a life that is governed by purity of heart. Christ thus teaches us here that holiness, consisting of purity of heart and life, is another distinguishing mark of God's people. The holiness that reveals itself in the lives of believers is not merely a cosmetic facade; rather, it proceeds from within.

We will now examine the second distinguishing mark of the Christian life by considering the nature, conduct, and blessedness of the pure in heart: namely, that they shall see God—the apex of experiential religion.

The Nature of the Pure in Heart

By addressing the purity of the heart, Christ is openly challenging the counterfeit religion of the Pharisees. All that mattered for them was their external appearance and conduct. They even boasted of this to others. When the appointed hour of prayer would arrive, they would find the most visible location so that they would have maximum exposure as they lifted their hands heavenward.

Christ, however, exposed their hypocrisy in blistering terms: "Woe unto you, scribes and Pharisees, hypocrites! for ye are like unto whited sepulchres, which indeed appear beautiful outward, but are within full of dead men's bones, and of all uncleanness" (Matt. 23:27). In Israel, a grave would often be above ground, and people would decorate those sepulchres. They would whitewash them to make them look as attractive as possible. But no matter what they did, it continued to be a grave. Christ declared the Pharisees to be such whitewashed sepulchres with nothing but the stench of death within. He contrasts this pharisaical holiness with a genuine purity of life that proceeds from purity within.

Yet by focusing on the inside, Christ is by no means implying that our external walk does not matter. I have dealt with people who have said to me, "Pastor, the outside doesn't matter; it doesn't matter what I look like. All that matters is the inside, for God only cares about the inside." Although there is an element of truth in this statement, it is also a flawed conclusion. The Beatitudes teach us that what is on the outside matters because it will inevitably be a manifestation of what transpires within. There is no such thing as someone being indwelt by the Holy Spirit who will not externally manifest the fruits of His indwelling ministry.

In other words, one cannot claim to be invisibly united to Christ when habitual, visible Christlikeness is absent. John 15 shows us that invisible union with Christ will become visible in godly living. Jesus underscored this by saying near the conclusion of His Sermon on the Mount, "Wherefore by their fruits ye shall know them. Not every one that saith unto me, Lord, Lord, shall enter into the kingdom of heaven; but he that doeth the will of my Father which is in heaven" (Matt. 7:20–21). According to Jesus, if one is not a habitual doer of His Father's will, one's verbal profession of His lordship is without substance.

When Christ proclaims the "pure in heart" blessed, He is referring to those who have a new and cleansed heart. What does the Bible mean by this? When Scripture speaks of the heart, it is referring to the spiritual core of our soul that governs everything we do. As our bodies cannot function without a physical heart, likewise our souls, the spiritual component of our being, cannot function without a spiritual heart.

When speaking of the soul, theologians distinguish between its three faculties: the mind, the affections, and the will. These three spiritual faculties intersect in the spiritual heart. Our heart governs what we think, love (desire), and do. However, the Bible also tells us that the heart of man, as a result of the fall, is utterly corrupt and is therefore nothing but a cesspool of moral wickedness, filth, and perversion. Jeremiah articulated this by declaring that "the heart is deceitful above all things, and desperately wicked: who can know it?"

(Jer. 17:9). Jeremiah is saying that the wickedness and perversion of the human heart is so radical and comprehensive that we cannot begin to fathom the extent of it.

Thus, when the news reports manifestations of human depravity, such as acts of terrorism or other acts of vile behavior, we need to understand that all of that evil originates in the desperately wicked human heart. Jesus exposed that wickedness in unsettling terms when He said, "For from within, out of the heart of men [this cesspool of iniquity], proceed evil thoughts, adulteries, fornications, murders, thefts, covetousness, wickedness, deceit, lasciviousness, an evil eye, blasphemy, pride, foolishness: all these evil things come from within, and defile the man" (Mark 7:21–23).

Such is the divine assessment of the natural human heart! Has this unsettling truth already become an experiential reality for you? Have you been awakened to the fact that your heart is desperately wicked? Have you learned to see that it is indeed a cesspool of iniquity? They who are poor in spirit will understand this experientially and will recognize the necessity of having a new and purified heart.

As sinners, we are therefore in need of a spiritual heart transplant. Some people have such serious heart disease that they cannot live much longer with their original heart. However, today we have the medical technology that makes it possible to replace a sick heart with a healthy one, thereby extending the life of such ailing persons. Spiritually speaking, unless we have a transplant, our natural heart will be the cause of our eternal perdition.

Ezekiel writes about such a spiritual heart transplant: "A new heart also will I give you, and a new spirit will I put within you: and I will take away the stony heart out of your flesh, and I will give you an heart of flesh" (Ezek. 36:26). Although we have a stony heart of flesh by nature, God here declares that He is going to replace it with a heart that is again inclined toward Him and His will.

When the Spirit of God renews us from within, we will begin to think, love, and act differently. Such radical inward renewal will affect our minds, our affections, and our wills. This inner renewal cannot remain hidden, for when our hearts are renewed, our lives will be also. When we begin to think differently, our desires and behaviors will change as well—all flowing out of that new heart. Just as the old heart is the fountain of all wickedness, so the new heart is the fountain of all genuine godliness.

The apostle Paul wrote to the Corinthians, "Know ye not that your body is the temple of the Holy Ghost which is in you, which ye have of God?" (1 Cor. 6:19). This is applicable to all believers. As the Holy of Holies of the temple was the place where God dwelt, so the renewed heart becomes the Holy of Holies where the Holy Spirit establishes His abiding presence, manifesting itself in a pure or holy life. By nature there is no such purity, for here Christ is referring to inner moral purity. He is thus pronouncing His benediction on those whose hearts have been cleansed, purified, and renewed.

Since Adam's heart was pure before he fell, he also lived a pure life. He had a pure love for God and his fellow man. The moment he fell, however, he lost that purity of heart and his life became corrupt. But thanks be to God that the Bible does not speak of only the first Adam! It also speaks of the second Adam, the Lord Jesus Christ, and His heart was pure in the fullest sense of the word. No iniquity was to be found in Him. As the second Adam, Christ was the beginning of a new humanity, and someday all those who are in Christ shall be like Him, having a perfectly pure heart.

Thus, Jesus is saying here that when someone is united to Him by the bond of saving faith, the result will be a purified heart, which will in turn become visible in a purified life. Paul writes in Titus 2:14 that Christ "gave himself for us, that he might redeem us from all iniquity, and purify unto himself a peculiar people, zealous of good works." The word *peculiar* here means distinguished or distinct, referring to a unique people who will be zealous of good works. Saving faith will bear visible fruit. True, Spirit-wrought Christianity cannot remain hidden and unnoticed.

In the marvelous work of regeneration, the Spirit of God will renew and cleanse the filthy heart of a sinner. We read in the book of Nehemiah that the enemies of Israel had invaded the temple and even occupied some of its chambers. Nehemiah was God's appointed instrument to cleanse the temple by expelling those who unlawfully occupied it. What did he do? He not only expelled the occupiers of the temple but also cleansed the chambers in which they had dwelt.

The Holy Spirit works in like fashion. He does what people do when they buy a house—perhaps an older one. How can one know that the home is being occupied by a new resident? Suddenly a large garbage container will appear in the driveway, and all sorts of things will be thrown out, for the new resident is renewing or restoring the house he purchased. Likewise, when the Holy Spirit establishes His blessed residence in the heart of a sinner, He will initiate the work of making our hearts holy again. And that inward renewal will manifest itself outwardly. But since true holiness proceeds from within, Jesus focuses on the heart in this beatitude, for a purified heart cannot but produce a purified life.

The Conduct of the Pure in Heart

The idea that true faith begins within and produces a holy life is expressed in Psalm 45:13: "The king's daughter is all glorious within." We can thus conclude that when the Spirit of Christ makes His abode in our hearts, we will begin to resemble Christ internally and externally. Simply put, purity of heart will manifest itself in Christlikeness, for holiness and Christlikeness are synonymous in Scripture. A genuine Christian will therefore in some measure begin to resemble the Lord Jesus Christ. If we profess to be a Christian, the members of our family should be able to see something of Christ in us. Those who live with us daily and know us intimately—our spouses, children, and siblings—should observe some tangible evidence of our purity of heart. If our transformation is real, those closest to us will detect it in our sanctified conduct.

Having been made pure in heart, the believer will increasingly become sensitive to all that is impure. Thus, we will become painfully aware of the abiding impurity that remains in our hearts. We will begin to understand what Solomon meant when he wrote in Proverbs 20:9, "Who can say, I have made my heart clean, I am pure from my sin?"

Hypersensitivity to sin is a mark of such Spirit-wrought purity of heart. True Christians will be concerned about and mourn over that which is known to God only. When a sinful thought arises in their hearts or crosses their minds, the pure in heart will groan inwardly and say, "Lord, forgive me for having even entertained such thoughts. Forgive me for having such a sinful desire." Can you relate to this? Have you learned to loathe yourself? God declares that such loathing will be one of the benefits of the covenant of grace: "Then shall ye remember your own evil ways, and your doings that were not good, and shall loathe yourselves in your own sight for your iniquities and for your abominations" (Ezek. 36:31).

When we begin to love God as a fruit of His love having been shed abroad in our hearts (Rom. 5:5)—when God, His Word, and His law become precious to us—we will begin to loathe all that is impure. The godly Paul therefore groaned, saying, "O wretched man that I am!" Here is the confession of a godly man who loathed the fact that he found himself doing that which he did not want to do, and that he failed to do what he was called to do.

Such continuous awareness of and loathing of sin, and a longing for all that is holy, is the distinguishing mark of the pure in heart. In Psalm 51, David supplicated, "Create in me a clean heart, O God; and renew a right spirit within me." Can you relate to this experientially? If you cannot, you are not a Christian. True saving faith will always be accompanied by a deep and painful consciousness of one's sinnership. That consciousness will drive the true believer to Christ and will make Him increasingly beautiful, desirable, precious, and altogether lovely. The Holy Spirit will teach us—repeatedly and increasingly—that as altogether unlovely sinners in ourselves we will only glory and trust in an altogether lovely Christ.

The Christian's purity of heart will exhibit itself in his or her life. First of all, believers will be sincere and upright in their talk and walk. We could thus rephrase this beatitude by saying that the blessed are they who are upright and sincere. A true Christian does not talk out of both sides of his mouth but rather earnestly strives to be sincere and upright. A Christian is a person in whom there is neither guile nor deceitfulness. Solomon addresses this when he speaks of the one who "loveth pureness of heart" (Prov. 22:11).

Second, the pure in heart will radically separate themselves from an impure world. Although that separation can be so deficient at times, there will nevertheless be a striving to be separate from this world. One of the great spiritual cancers of North American Christianity is conformity to the world. What damage that has inflicted on the church of Jesus Christ! However, despite the sinful compromises of even the godly, their inward purity, as a result of the indwelling Spirit of purity, will reassert itself by a sincere endeavor to be and remain separate from this world. James 1:27 teaches plainly that one of the components of pure religion is to keep oneself "unspotted from the world." Dear reader, is it also your desire, by grace, to keep yourself unspotted from the world?

Third, in addition to being sincere in talk and walk and endeavoring to be separate from the world, the pure in heart have no tolerance for sin, because God's beloved Son had to die on the cross for sin—indeed, even for their sin. Therefore, when the love of God is shed abroad in our hearts, we will also have no tolerance for sin. The apostle Paul expressed this strikingly in Acts 24:16: "And herein do I exercise myself, to have always a conscience void to offence toward God, and toward men." In essence, Paul is saying that he went out of his way each day to cleanse or purify his conscience and thus be void of offense toward God and his fellow man. That is a mark of being pure in heart!

Finally, purity of heart reveals itself in genuine and unconditional love for one's neighbor. In 1 Timothy 1:5 we read, "Now the end of the commandment is charity out of a pure heart." There you have it: love proceeding from a pure heart, a good conscience, and a faith unfeigned. Peter exhorts, "See that ye love one another with a pure heart fervently" (1 Peter 1:22).

Living a holy life means that, by the grace of Christ, we strive to be conformed to Christ, following in the footsteps of the Master. We will then prayerfully strive to live an obedient life—not to earn God's favor but rather to demonstrate our love for the One who has bestowed His favor on us. Jesus therefore said, "If ye love me, keep my commandments" (John 14:15). To love the Lord Jesus Christ means that we will also take all of His words seriously. To put it differently, all who love the Living Word will seek to honor His written Word. Dear reader, do you take God's Word seriously—all of it? Is that the pure desire of your heart?

Thus, the core desire of the pure in heart, of every true Christian, will be walking with and living in fellowship with

God. Walking with God means to have a longing to be near to Him, a longing for His presence, a longing to have communion with Him, and a longing to behold Him as He has revealed Himself in His Word. Jesus says that the pure in heart will therefore see God. They hunger and thirst after righteousness, which ultimately means they yearn after God Himself. David expresses this by saying in Psalm 42:1, "As the hart panteth after the water brooks, so panteth my soul after thee, O God." Dear reader, do you desire to see God—to walk with Him and be near to Him? Do you long to live in fellowship and communion with Him? If that is the case, Christ says here that you will be satisfied, for you will see God.

The Blessedness of the Pure in Heart

In the culture of Jesus' day, it was almost impossible for an ordinary citizen to see the king. You would need a special invitation, and special arrangements would have to be made for entering into the very presence of the king. However, Christ says to the pure in heart, to those who hunger and thirst after righteousness, that it will be their privilege to see God, who, for Christ's sake, will admit them into His blessed presence.

What does it mean for the pure in heart to see God? Since God is a Spirit, we cannot see Him in His spiritual essence with our physical eyes. Christ speaks here of the seeing of faith—of beholding God as He has revealed Himself in His Word. To see Him means that they will delight themselves in seeing His revealed perfections and will enjoy intimate fellowship with Him. To see God means to know Him intimately and to live in fellowship and communion with Him. Such was

Adam's privilege! He was privileged to see God every morning and every evening when God would meet with him in the cool of the day. Adam saw God; that is, he walked and lived with Him, enjoying daily communion with Him.

As a result of the fall, man was cast out of God's presence. A holy God could no longer permit an unholy man to see Him. However, in Jesus Christ, God has paved the way whereby a sinner can see Him again in the person of His only begotten Son. Paul describes this beautifully in 2 Corinthians 4:6: "For God, who commanded the light to shine out of darkness, hath shined in our hearts, to give the light of the knowledge of the glory of God in the face of Jesus Christ." We can now see God in His only begotten Son, the Living Word. To behold Christ is to behold His Father. Christ affirmed this emphatically by saying, "He that hath seen me hath seen the Father" (John 14:9). Jesus is the revelation of the Father: the brightness of His glory and the express image of His person (Heb. 1:3).

Nothing is sweeter than to behold God in Christ! The sweetest moments in the lives of believers are when they may see something of His incomparable glory and beauty. In Christ, the invisible God becomes visible, for "no man hath seen God at any time, the only begotten Son, which is in the bosom of the Father, he hath declared him" (John 1:18).

However, in this beatitude Jesus makes it clear that the privilege of seeing God experientially is intimately connected to a holy life. Consequently, when a Christian lives carelessly and backslides—when he neither walks with God nor has daily communion with Him—he is living in darkness and should not expect to see God. Second Peter 1:9 states, "But he that lacketh these things is blind, and cannot see afar off, and hath forgotten that he was purged from his old sins." Simply put, the Christian will lose his assurance. God will not tolerate sin in the lives of His people.

The privilege of enjoying God and of seeing Him is reserved for those who walk in holiness. Peter therefore also said, "If these things be in you, and abound, they make you that ye shall neither be barren nor unfruitful in the knowledge of our Lord Jesus Christ" (2 Peter 1:8). Psalm 97:11 declares that "[l]ight is sown for the righteous, and gladness for the upright [pure] in heart." That does not mean, however, that salvation is by works. Rather, if you strive by God's grace to deal with sin in your life and crucify your flesh, and if you prayerfully and sincerely endeavor to order your life according to His Word, you will see Him and experience His favor.

In this life, the experiential seeing of God is an interrupted experience, for God will hide His face from us when we play fast and loose with sin. He wants to teach us to take sin seriously and to develop in us a hypersensitivity toward sin. One of the means by which He achieves this is by withdrawing the sense of His presence and His favor within our soul until we return to Him in the way of repentance and again seek His face.

Part of maintaining purity of heart is also making sure that there are no unresolved conflicts in our lives. Jesus says later in His sermon that one should not come to the altar for worship if there is unresolved conflict with one's neighbor. In short, we must resolve such conflict before coming into God's presence, for only the pure in heart will see God.

Let me stress again that God is not asking us to come before Him with a righteousness of our own making. Rather, He wants us to understand that since He is holy, He has zero tolerance for sin. Thus, He wants His people to have zero tolerance for sin as well. Peter affirms this when he writes, "But as he which hath called you is holy, so be ye holy in all manner of conversation; because it is written, Be ye holy; for I am holy" (1 Peter 1:15–16).

The awareness of this truth makes the following promise so exceedingly precious to the pure in heart: "If we confess our sins, he is faithful and just to forgive us our sins, and to cleanse us from all unrighteousness" (1 John 1:9). Only when we do so faithfully and consistently will we be able to maintain purity of heart and experience God's favor. John, being desirous that believers would live in the enjoyment of seeing God, therefore hastens to add, "If any man sin, we have an advocate with the Father, Jesus Christ the righteous: and he is the propitiation for our sins" (1 John 2:1–2).

However, the day will come, dear believer, when you will always see Him. The same apostle John tells us, "We know that, when he shall appear, we shall be like him; for we shall see him as he is" (1 John 3:2). Then we will see Christ as we have never seen Him before, and we will at last be like Him. Then we will have perfectly pure hearts and live perfectly pure lives.

David says in Psalm 17:15, "As for me, I will behold thy face in righteousness: I shall be satisfied, when I awake, with thy likeness." Job firmly believed that as well! He said, "In my flesh shall I see God" (Job 19:26). In Revelation 22:3–4, we find these wonderful words, "And there shall be no more curse: but the throne of God and of the Lamb shall be in it; and his servants shall serve him: and they shall see his face." They shall see God indeed! That will be the privilege and supreme happiness of heaven: to see God in Christ. God's people, the pure in heart, will always and forever behold God in the person of the Lord Jesus Christ.

Dear reader, do you long for that? Do you recognize yourself in this beatitude? Do you belong to the pure in heart? John puts it this way in 1 John 3:3: "Every man that hath this hope in him purifieth himself, even as he is pure." Proverbs 20:11 says, "Even a child is known by his doings, whether his work be pure, and whether it be right." After all, actions speak louder than words!

Dear believer, I know how often you grieve about your impurity and how you loathe it! But be encouraged. Let the Spirit of God direct you to look outside of yourself to Christ. Continue to take refuge to Him as a poor and needy sinner in yourself, expecting your entire salvation from Him alone. How comforting indeed is the astounding truth expressed by the apostle Paul: "But of him are ye in Christ Jesus, who of God is made unto us wisdom, and righteousness, and sanctification, and redemption" (1 Cor. 1:30). He is the all in all of the pure in heart!

Dear reader, have you, by faith, seen God in Christ, His beloved Son? There will be a day in which we will all see Him coming in great glory on the clouds. Then "every eye shall see him, and they also which pierced him: and all kindreds of the earth shall wail because of him" (Rev. 1:7). If that is the first time you see Him, you will wish you had never seen Him, for He will then be coming as the Judge of all the earth. You will then see Him in His wrath and hear Him saying, "Depart from me, ye cursed, into everlasting fire, prepared for the devil and his angels" (Matt. 25:41). God forbid that the judgment day is the first time you see God!

Now is the accepted time and the day of salvation to seek the God who has revealed Himself in the gospel, specifically in His only begotten Son, the Lord Jesus Christ. If you have never sought Him, seek this precious Savior today, for He came to seek and to save sinners whose hearts are desperately wicked. He came to give Himself as a ransom for many, and His precious blood will cleanse the vilest sinner from all sin.

Finally, dear believer, may you experience, and continue to experience, the truth of this beatitude: "Blessed are the pure in heart: for they shall see God."

Discussion Questions

1. By pronouncing the pure in heart as being blessed, how did Christ challenge the phony piety of the Pharisees?

2. How do the three faculties of the soul intersect in the spiritual heart of man, and how does this manifest itself in one's life—before and after regeneration?

3. How does purity of heart flow out of being united to Christ by faith?

4. What is meant by the expression that the regenerate heart of the believer is the Holy of Holies of the temple of the Holy Spirit?

5. What experiential awareness will be generated by being pure of heart? What connection is there with the second beatitude regarding mourning?

6. How does purity of heart manifest itself in the Christian's walk or conversation?

7. What is meant by "seeing God"? And why is this the unique privilege of the pure in heart?

8. What vital connection is there between seeing God and the Lord Jesus Christ?

9. What lesson does God teach His children by hiding His face when they regard sin in their hearts?

10. What provision has God made so that His children may see Him daily? When will this become an uninterrupted reality (Rev. 22:3–4)?

Chapter 7

GOD'S CHILDREN ARE PEACEMAKERS

Blessed are the peacemakers: for they shall be called the children of God.

—MATTHEW 5:9

We will now focus on the seventh trait of Christ's portrait of the Christian: "Blessed are the peacemakers." This seventh beatitude is literally the bottom line of Christ's description of the citizens of His spiritual kingdom. Specifically, it is the cumulative assessment of His entire verbal portrait, for here Jesus says that all who manifest these spiritual traits shall be called the children of God. As Thomas Watson said, "This is the seventh step of the golden ladder which leads to blessedness."[1]

We will examine this final trait by discussing the identity, conduct, and blessedness of the peacemakers, for "they shall be called the children of God."

---

1. Thomas Watson, *The Beatitudes* (Edinburgh: Banner of Truth, 1975), 204.

The Peacemaker's Identity

The last three beatitudes—being merciful, pure in heart, and peacemakers—are a reflection of God's character. Christ said, "Be ye therefore merciful, as your Father also is merciful" (Luke 6:36). Peter summarizes God's repeated exhortation to His covenant people, saying, "Be ye holy; for I am holy" (1 Peter 1:16). The obvious inference is that a holy God has a holy people.

Peacemaking is also a reflection of God's character. Christ highlights that remarkably in this beatitude by saying that peacemakers "are the children of God." The disposition and conduct of the citizens of His kingdom will be a faint yet unmistakable reflection of God's character. In a human family, children will manifest the physical and/or character traits of their parents. Christ is saying here that this is analogous to God's spiritual family, for the children of God will reflect the character of their heavenly Father. Indeed, God Himself is the ultimate Author of peace.

We must now proceed to define peace. Positively, peace expresses a state of harmony; negatively, it is a state void of all discord. When God created the universe in Genesis 1 and 2, perfect peace prevailed everywhere. There was perfect harmony between God and men, between Adam and Eve, between our first parents and the animal world, and between earth and the rest of the universe. The entire universe was a marvel of flawless integration and exquisite harmony.

However, that wondrous fabric of peace was rudely disrupted and torn asunder as a result of sin. Adam and Eve, our highly favored and privileged first parents, believed Satan's lie and disobeyed the express command of their loving heavenly Father. In so doing, they filed for a spiritual divorce, which tragically severed the harmonious love relationship between God and themselves. From that moment on, peace vanished from the earth.

Yet amazingly, before God expelled Adam and Eve from the garden of Eden, He sued for peace! When He came in the cool of the day for His daily encounter of fellowship with them, He called His disobedient children out of hiding, doing so not to destroy them but rather to offer them peace. No sooner had Adam and Eve declared war and joined ranks with God's archenemy, Satan, than God revealed Himself immediately to them as the great Peacemaker, saying to them (and I paraphrase), "You have now forged a friendship with Satan. However, I am going to break that friendship. 'I will put enmity between thee and the woman, and between thy seed and her seed; it shall bruise thy head, and thou shalt bruise his heel' (Gen. 3:15). That is, in the fullness of time, I will send the seed of the woman through whom I will bring you back into a peaceful relationship with Myself—through whom I am going to restore peace and harmony."

Thus, Jesus, the eternal Son of God, was born as the Seed of the Woman, for "when the fulness of the time was come, God sent forth his Son, made of a woman, made under the law, to redeem them that were under the law, that we might receive the adoption of sons" (Gal. 4:4–5). Heaven itself affirmed the glorious purpose of His blessed incarnation when the angels burst on the scene in the fields of Ephrata, praising God by saying, "Glory to God in the highest, and on earth peace, good will toward men" (Luke 2:14).

Their words make clear that as a result of Jesus' birth, the triune God will be supremely glorified, peace on earth will be restored, and there will be good will toward men—fallen and rebellious sons and daughters of Adam! These words could actually be rephrased as saying that God will bestow peace on men of His good pleasure—the wording of the Dutch rendition of the Bible. Thus, as the great Peacemaker, God the Father sent His beloved Son into the world to execute His eternal counsel of peace. He so loved a world of fallen and rebellious men that He gave His only begotten Son as the ultimate expression of that love. He forsook His Son on the cross so that, on the basis of Christ's perfect and atoning sacrifice, He can freely proffer peace and pardon to hell-worthy sons and daughters of Adam.

God is thus the great Peacemaker! In His eternal counsel of peace He has eternally purposed that all that is destroyed through sin should be restored in and through the Lord Jesus Christ. The wondrous outcome of the redemption conceived in the heart of the triune God is that He will sovereignly restore sinners into a harmonious relationship with Himself. Such is indeed the promise of the gospel, for to those who believe in His Son, He declares in essence, "Though you have been at war with Me, because you have trusted in My Son and His finished work, I will receive you into a peaceful relationship with Myself."

Therefore, all who by grace and faith have embraced the Lord Jesus Christ will increasingly begin to experience a peace that passes all understanding. In fact, they will increasingly understand that Christ is the embodiment of that peace. The apostle Paul declares plainly: "For he is our peace, who hath made both one, and hath broken down the middle wall of partition between us" (Eph. 2:14). In verse 17, he continues by saying that Christ "came and preached peace to you which were afar off, and to them that were nigh."

What a wonder indeed that God is the great peace *Maker*! He did not wait for us to take the initiative. If He would have waited for us, there would never have been peace on earth, for by nature we are not at all interested in being at peace with our Creator. Instead, a fallen and rebellious humanity lives in a state of constant warfare with God.

Thanks be to God that He took the initiative in eternity and in the fullness of time! And, dear believer, He also took the initiative when He graciously dealt with your soul. When He found you, He did not find you as a seeker after God. Instead, He found you as an enemy, as an unbeliever, as a servant of sin, and as an ally of Satan. But it is also true for you what Paul wrote to the Ephesians: "But God, who is rich in mercy, for his great love wherewith he loved us, even when we were dead in sins, hath quickened us together with Christ" (Eph. 2:4–5). As the great and omnipotent Peacemaker, He lovingly, graciously, and irresistibly drew you to Himself and made peace with you.

In this seventh beatitude, Christ therefore posits that those with whom God has made peace (on the basis of His merits) will begin to show forth the fruit of being peacemakers themselves. He teaches that this is the ultimate affirmation that the citizens of His kingdom are indeed the children of God. Their conduct as peacemakers is a reflection of their Father's character.

The trait of such spiritual peacemaking will thus *never* be found in unregenerate men. Ever since we fell in Adam, we have been warmongers and troublemakers. As fallen human beings, we are inclined to hate God and our neighbor (Rom. 1:30; Titus 3:3). This world has therefore always been filled with war between nations, people, and families. By nature, we are lovers of ourselves, making trouble with anyone who either gets in our way or challenges us. Christ, however, says that when one becomes a citizen of His kingdom, he will become a peacemaker. The children of God are a people who, as a fruit of the marvelous regenerating work of the Holy Spirit, have been transformed from troublemakers into peacemakers.

What sort of people are we? Are we peacemakers or troublemakers? Scripture says of the ungodly, "And the way of peace have they not known" (Rom. 3:17). The mark of the unbeliever is that he does not know the way of peace. In Titus 3:3, Paul acknowledges, "For we ourselves also were sometimes foolish, disobedient, deceived, serving divers lusts and pleasures, living in malice and envy, hateful, and hating one another." Dear believer, Paul would also say to us, "and such were some of you" (1 Cor. 6:11). When the Spirit of God regenerates us, however, making us a new creature in Christ by uniting us to Him, He will also commence the restoration of God's image in us.

When vertical peace is restored between God and our soul, such Spirit-wrought peace will also begin to manifest itself horizontally. James therefore concludes, "But the wisdom that is from above is first pure, then peaceable, gentle, and easy to be entreated, full of mercy and good fruits, without partiality, and without hypocrisy" (James 3:17). Please take notice of the textual connection between purity and peacemaking: first pure, then peaceable! Christ is thus saying that one of the most prominent marks of holiness or godliness (Christlikeness!) will be that we are peacemakers who endeavor to live in harmony with both God and our fellow man. Since union with Christ will always produce likeness to Christ, our spiritual union to the Peacemaker Himself will transform us into peacemakers. Consequently, Paul lists this as one of the fruits of the Spirit when he writes, "But the fruit of the Spirit is love, joy, peace, longsuffering, gentleness, goodness, faith" (Gal. 5:22).

The Peacemaker's Conduct

Having established the identity of the peacemaker, we will now focus on the conduct of the peacemaker. Let me begin by emphasizing that Christ does *not* say, "Blessed are the peace lovers." Rather, He says, "Blessed are the peace*makers*." Thus, the calling of the Christian is to take the initiative in the pursuit of peace. To be Christlike means that we will go out of our way to take the initiative toward our neighbor, making sure that we live in harmony with our fellow man. Peacemakers are called to make the first move toward reconciliation. Paul makes that point explicitly in Romans 12:18, saying, "If it be possible, as much as lieth in you, live peaceably with all men." That's remarkable language! Paul is saying that if there is any discord in our relationships, we should have a clear conscience before God that we are not the perpetrators and that we have done everything in our power to resolve any residual conflict.

In his commentary on Matthew 5:9, John Calvin argues, "By peacemakers Jesus means those who not only seek peace and avoid quarrels as far as lies in their power but who also labor to settle differences among others, who advise all men to live at peace and take away every occasion of hatred and strife." That's what it means to be a peacemaker!

What are some of the qualities of the peacemaker? The parallel structure of the Beatitudes immediately yields the first quality: one has to be meek—and thus be of a humble disposition. Here also the inward disposition of the Christian will manifest itself outwardly. Discord between people is frequently fueled by ugly, self-seeking, and self-serving pride. Troublemaking is one of the wretched fruits of our proud and ungodly flesh. Even believers must painfully and shamefully admit that when their flesh gets the upper hand, they will also behave as troublemakers rather than peacemakers.

When, however, the Spirit of God and His grace prevail, and when we are thus humbled before God, we cannot possibly remain proud and arrogant. Instead, we will become meek (not weak!). And when we are meek, we will focus on the virtues of others rather than on their vices. Sadly, we are naturally inclined to do the opposite, and gossip continues to flourish, even in the church.

A peacemaker, on the contrary, will have a great measure of tolerance toward the faults and failures of others. He will not be easily offended. He will defy the wisdom of this world by being willing to take the lowest place. A peacemaker, being poor in spirit, will be painfully conscious of his own sinfulness. Peacemakers are also very careful as to how they use their tongue. So much trouble and discord is caused by the abuse of our tongues! A peacemaker learns to bite his tongue, especially at critical moments, learning that at times it is best to remain silent.

Such peacemaking begins at home. That means, first and foremost, that husbands and wives need to be peacemakers rather than troublemakers. What often precipitates marital conflict? Is it not our wretched and carnal tendency to be troublemakers rather than peacemakers? Peacemaking in our marriages therefore means that husbands must take the initiative to be at peace with their wives, making certain that their relationship functions harmoniously. The task of a godly wife will be to take the initiative toward being at peace with her husband. When that happens, marital peace and harmony will flourish. To make that happen, we must exercise ourselves in taking the initiative and in taking the lowest place. To be a Christlike spouse, one must be willing to be the least. Blessed indeed are the marital peacemakers!

This calling to be peacemakers also applies to other family relationships. We need to examine ourselves here as well. Are there any unresolved conflicts with any members of either your immediate or extended family? If so, have you done everything in your power to resolve them? Have you been a peacemaker in earnestly endeavoring to restore those challenged relationships? Consider what Solomon says in Proverbs 6:16–19: "These six things doth the LORD hate: yea, seven are an abomination unto him." The last thing mentioned is "he that soweth discord among brethren." God hates troublemaking because He is the Peacemaker!

God forbid that we would ever be guilty of sowing discord among brethren! Hebrews 12:14 says, "Follow peace with all men, and holiness, without which no man shall see the Lord." Again, following peace with all men clearly implies that the initiative must be ours. In Romans 13:8, Paul admonishes, "Owe no man any thing, but to love one another: for he that loveth another hath fulfilled the law." An essential component of loving your neighbor as yourself is to be a peacemaker.

Proverbs 20:3 teaches us that "it is an honor for a man to cease from strife." How contrary this is to our natural inclination! The world's philosophy (conceived in carnal hearts) is that in any conflict you must strive to come out on top. The motto of our carnal flesh is "Don't stop fighting and don't stop quarreling until you have won the day." However, the Bible says, "It is an honor for a man to cease from strife." It is an honor to step away from trouble and to do everything we can to douse the fires of contention and conflict. Paul exhorts us very plainly to do so, saying, "God hath called us to peace" (1 Cor. 7:15). That is our sacred calling as Christians!

When we begin to grasp what God as the great Peacemaker has achieved for us through the mediatorial work of His only begotten Son, it will become visible in our lives and in our relationships that we are also peacemakers. Therefore Christ says with profound intent and purpose that peacemakers "shall be called the children of God." He thereby teaches that true Christianity will be relational in nature, for God is a relational Being. After all, the Trinity is a relationship between the Father and the Son, who love each other infinitely and comprehensively in the person of the Holy Spirit. Consequently, to have been created by the triune God as His image bearers means that He created us as relational beings. The essence of God's law therefore demands that our relationship with God and our relationship with our fellow man be governed by love (Matt. 22:37–40). Thus, true peace with God in Christ must translate into peace with one's neighbor.

The Peacemaker's Blessedness

In Greek, there are two words that we translate as "child." One (*teknon*) refers to birth and a child's genetic connection with his biological parents. The other word (*huios*) communicates that a child will reflect his parents' character. Thus, having been born of our parents, we will also have inherited something of their character. And so it is in the kingdom of heaven. When we are born of God, we will begin to reflect His character. Paul expresses this in Romans 8:14: "For as many as are led by the Spirit of God, they are the sons of God."

The same word is used here in Matthew 5:9. Thus, a born-again child of God will in some measure begin to resemble his heavenly Father. Jesus is teaching here that peacemakers in particular will prove themselves to be "the sons of God." One could even paraphrase His words as follows: peacemakers will be owned by God as His children, and He will do so because peacemaking so eminently reflects His character.

It should be understood, however, that the identification of being the children of God applies ultimately to all seven beatitudes. As has been stated before, their structure is progressive and cumulative. He who is poor in spirit will also mourn; he who mourns over sin will also be meek; and he who is consequently meek will also hunger and thirst after righteousness and be filled. This, in turn, as we have repeatedly asserted, will yield a disposition of being merciful to others, of being pure in heart, and, finally, of being a peacemaker.

In this final descriptive beatitude, Jesus in effect says, "To whom all of this applies, and of whom all of this is true, they, and they alone, shall be called the children of God. They reflect the character of My and their heavenly Father." To be designated as a child of God is such an extraordinary privilege!

In contrast, Jesus said to the Pharisees, "You are of your father the devil" (John 8:44). By nature, we resemble Satan rather than God, for Satan is the author of all trouble and discord. As the prince of this world, he is also the great troublemaker of this world. Satan disrupted the peaceful harmony that we had between God and our fellow man. He delights in stoking the fires of contention and discord, and thus we resemble him when we behave as troublemakers.

When young children visit relatives or friends, parents will often say, "Make sure you behave yourself!" That means, while you are visiting, you must make sure that you behave yourself in such a way that you will not dishonor our name and reputation as parents. Parents say this because they recognize that their children's behavior will reflect in some measure who they are. This is also applicable to the household of God. We cannot claim to be children of God unless we, in some measure, begin to conduct ourselves as such. If natural children have a positive obligation to love, honor, and respect their parents and a negative obligation neither to embarrass nor dishonor them by their conduct, how much more this ought to be practiced in the spiritual household of God!

God has indeed called us to peace. Having said that, we need to recognize that none of us reflects Christ's portrait of the Christian perfectly. No Christian in this life will always and consistently behave as a peacemaker. The recognition of that fact will grieve the child of God, for the desire of the new man is after holiness and righteousness. The life of the true Christian will therefore be one of spiritual warfare—a continuous battle between the new man and the old man. The old man still residing in the believer (his flesh) is as ugly as the flesh of the ungodly. Flesh is flesh, and that flesh must be crucified and put to death.

Sadly, there are occasions when our flesh gets the upper hand and we behave as troublemakers rather than peacemakers. How we should grieve over this! When such is the case, the grieved Spirit of God dwelling in believers will convict them and strive with them until they acknowledge this and make every effort to resolve conflict. When that happens, the new man will be manifesting itself. Therefore, Christians may not say, "Well, you will just have to take me the way I am." Instead, we need to acknowledge that we are called to peace. That calling is never optional for a Christian!

Therefore, the more we abide in Christ and walk with Him, the more we will begin to resemble Him. In John 15:4–5, Jesus stresses this point, saying, "Abide in me, and I in you. As the branch cannot bear fruit of itself, except it abide in the vine; no more can ye, except ye abide in me. I am the vine, ye are the branches: He that abideth in me, and I in him, the same bringeth forth much fruit: for without me ye can do nothing." He is saying, so to speak, "Don't just come to Me. You must also abide with Me. You must stay with Me, walk with Me, and live in fellowship with Me." We cannot prosper in the Christian life unless we experientially abide in Christ.

Spending time daily in God's Word and in prayer is therefore neither an option nor a luxury for the Christian— it is a necessity. When we become careless in our Christian walk, we will drift away from Christ. What happens when we no longer abide in Him? The old man begins to reassert itself again. When we neglect our new man, the old man will gain in strength, and some of the ugly fruits of the flesh will begin to manifest themselves again. Remember, however, that when we act in the flesh, we will bring dishonor on God and the Lord Jesus Christ, who gave Himself as a ransom for us so that we might be at peace with our Maker and our fellow man.

How seriously we must therefore be in our calling as peacemakers! Knowing how weak we are in ourselves, Jesus emphatically states in John 15:5, "Without me ye can do nothing." We need to interpret these often-misquoted words in their context. Jesus is saying (and I paraphrase), "Without abiding in Me, you cannot bear a single fruit, and therefore you must abide in Me. If you abide in me and I in you, you shall bear much fruit." Christ is using this negation to affirm positively that everything we need to live the Christian life is to be found only in Him. Christian, you must therefore daily abide in Jesus, for when you do, He will also abide in you, and you will bear much fruit. He is the Fountain and Sustainer of all spiritual life.

In this seventh beatitude, Christ has given us the "bottom line" of His spiritual portrait: are we peacemakers or are we troublemakers? We will be one of the two. As Thomas Watson said, "It is Satan who kindles the fires of contention in men's hearts and then stands and warms himself at the fire."[2] Therefore, we who profess to be God's children ought not to give Satan such an opportunity, for we are called to be peacemakers. Paul writes, "Let us therefore follow after the things which make for peace, and things wherewith one may edify another" (Rom. 14:19). First John 3:10 affirms, "In this the children of God are manifest, and the children of the devil." Thus, we should either go out of our way to resolve conflict or else we should stop calling ourselves Christians. We cannot have it both ways!

2. Watson, *Beatitudes*, 209.

Discussion Questions

1. What statement in the seventh beatitude confirms that the order of the Beatitudes is progressive and cumulative?

2. Define peace. How did this manifest itself before the fall?

3. How did God prove Himself to be the great Peacemaker in the Garden of Eden and at the cross?

4. Why is peacemaking such remarkable evidence of the supernatural and transforming grace of God in the heart of a sinner?

5. What important truth is Christ emphasizing by identifying God's children as peace*makers* rather than peace *lovers*?

6. What precisely does Christ mean when He designates peacemakers as *children* of God?

7. Why is there no greater privilege imaginable than to be called *a child of God*?

8. How are the last three beatitudes all a reflection of God's character?

9. What connection is there between manifesting the seven traits of Christ's spiritual portrait and abiding in Christ (John 15)?

10. Why is it so encouraging and liberating for the believer that progressive sanctification is not becoming what we must be but rather becoming what we already are in Christ positionally?

CONCLUSION

In this book, we have engaged in a rather in-depth examination and analysis of Christ's perfect portrait of the Christian. Do you in some measure recognize yourself in this portrait? Again, none of us will ever reflect that portrait perfectly. Having said that, however, as deficient and feeble as our spiritual life may at times be, if you are a Christian, the seven traits of Christ's portrait will manifest themselves. To put it simply, the Beatitudes are a complete package—it is all or nothing. When the Spirit of God works in us, He will produce all seven of these marks: poverty in spirit, mournfulness, meekness, a hunger and thirst after righteousness, mercy, purity in heart (and life!), and peacemaking.

The world will respond to such genuine Christians with hatred and persecution. Christ therefore appends to these seven beatitudes the eighth and final beatitude: "Blessed are they which are persecuted for righteousness' sake: for theirs is the kingdom of heaven. Blessed are ye, when men shall revile you, and persecute you, and shall say all manner of evil against you falsely, for my sake. Rejoice, and be exceeding glad: for great is your reward in heaven: for so persecuted they the prophets which were before you" (Matt. 5:10–12).

Christ calls blessed those whose godliness is such that the world recognizes it and responds to it with hatred. Blessed are they who so resemble their heavenly Father that the world will grudgingly acknowledge it as well. An ungodly world will tolerate nominal and counterfeit Christianity. After all, such "Christians" pose no threat, for they live in conformity to the world's agenda. But the genuine and vital Christianity articulated by Christ in the Beatitudes will expose and condemn the wickedness of an ungodly world and thus provoke persecution. What a badge of honor it is when we so resemble Christ that the world will want to eliminate us as well!

Blessed indeed are they who may recognize themselves in Christ's portrait of the Christian. However, dear reader, if that is not yet your portrait, you are still subject to God's curse! To be subject to God's curse means that the execution of His wrath on you is inescapable. You will be condemned by the Judge of all the earth—that is, unless you repent and believe in His beloved Son, the Lord Jesus Christ. There is no other name given under heaven among men whereby you must and can be saved (Acts 4:12)! In Christ, God is still willing to make peace with you, and in the gospel He is therefore proffering peace and pardon to you. Do not harden your heart; rather, come to the God and Father of the Lord Jesus Christ, who, as the great Peacemaker and for the sake of His Son, is freely and unconditionally offering His peace to you. In Jesus, the Father is ready to pardon the vilest sinner (Ps. 86:5)!

Dear children of God, blessed indeed are the peacemakers, whose only hope is in the Prince of Peace—who also is our peace! Let me therefore end with the words of the apostle Paul in 2 Corinthians 13:11: "Finally, brethren, farewell. Be perfect, be of good comfort, be of one mind, live in peace; and the God of love and peace shall be with you."

SELECTED
BIBLIOGRAPHY

Barnes, Albert. *Notes on the Gospels of Matthew and Mark.*
    Edinburgh: Gall & Inglis, n.d.

Burroughs, Jeremiah. *The Saints' Happiness: Lectures on the
    Beatitudes.* Beaver Falls, PA: Soli Deo Gloria Publica-
    tions, n.d.

Calvin, John. *Commentary on a Harmony of the Evangelists:
    Matthew, Mark, Luke, vol. 1.* Grand Rapids, MI: Baker,
    1979.

Doriani, Daniel M. *The Sermon on the Mount.* Phillipsburg,
    NJ: P&R Publishing, 2006.

Ferguson, Sinclair B. *The Sermon on the Mount: Kingdom Life
    in a Fallen World.* Carlisle, PA: Banner of Truth, 2006.

Gangar, Kuldip Singh. *Devotional Commentary on the Gospel
    of Matthew.* Calgary, AB: Free Reformed Publications,
    2014.

Gill, John. *Commentary on the Holy Scriptures.* 6 vols. Grand
    Rapids, MI: Baker, 1980.

Grosheide, F. W. *Het Heilig Evangelie Volgens Mattheus* [The
    Holy Gospel according to Matthew]. Kampen, the
    Netherlands: J. H. Kok, 1954.

Hendriksen, William. *New Testament Commentary: Matthew.*
    Grand Rapids, MI: Baker, 1973.

Henry, Matthew. *Commentary on the Whole Bible*. Peabody, MA: Hendrickson Publishers, 2003.

Jamieson, Robert, ed. *Commentary Critical and Explanatory on the Whole Bible*. Grand Rapids, MI: Zondervan, n.d.

Lloyd-Jones, D. Martin. *Studies in the Sermon on the Mount*. Grand Rapids, MI: Eerdmans, 1976.

Pink, Arthur W. *An Exposition of the Sermon on the Mount*. Grand Rapids, MI: Baker, 1970.

Poole, Matthew. *Commentary on the Holy Bible*. 3 vols. Carlisle, PA: Banner of Truth, 1990.

Ridderbos, N. H. *Korte Verklaring der Heilige Schrift: Mattheus* [Concise Exposition of the Holy Scriptures: Matthew]. Kampen, the Netherlands: J. H. Kok, 1952.

Rienecker, Fritz. *Das Evangelium des Matthäus: Wuppentaler Studienbibel* [The Gospel of Matthew: Wuppentaler Study Bible]. Wuppertal, Germany: R. Brockhaus Verlag, 1974.

Robertson, Archibald T. *Word Pictures in the New Testament: Matthew & Mark*. Nashville, TN: Broadman Press, 1930.

Ryle, J. C. *Expository Thoughts on Matthew*. Carlisle, PA: Banner of Truth, 2001.

Scott, Thomas. *Commentary on the Holy Bible*. 6 vols. New York: Samuel T. Armstrong and Crocker & Brewster, 1835.

Spurgeon, Charles H. *Commentary on Matthew: The Gospel of the Kingdom*. Carlisle, PA: Banner of Truth, 2013.

Steinberger, Georg. *Kleine Lichter auf den Weg der Nachfolge* [*Small Lights upon the Pathway of Obedience*]. Stuttgart, Germany: Christliches Verlagshaus, 1986.

Watson, Thomas. *The Beatitudes: An Exposition of Matthew 5:1–12*. Carlisle, PA: Banner of Truth, 1975.